The Vegetarian Slow Cooker Cookbook

The Vegetarian Slow Cooker Cookbook

150 Unbeatably Tasty Recipes

By Jackie Collis

Table of Contents

Side Dish Recipes 117

Introduction

Do you struggle to find the time or energy to cook a healthy and tasty meal at the end of a long day? If you want a quick solution to this problem, then a slow cooker could be your new best friend.

I know what you're thinking. How is a "slow" cooker going to save me time? Well, the appeal of a slow cooker is its simplicity. Turn it on, add the ingredients, and go about your business until you're ready to eat. There's no slaving over a stove, keeping an eye on burning ingredients or worrying about overflowing hot water. Sounds too good to be true doesn't it? Well, it isn't!

This is exactly why the popularity of slow cookers has risen exponentially over recent years. A kitchen tool that was once resigned to making stews and casseroles now offers a huge amount of variety and flexibility for every type of diet. The principle, however, has always remained the same. The food is cooked in a ceramic bowl at a low temperature for a longer duration, enhancing the flavor of dishes without the effort.

With modern lifestyles hectic at the best of times, who wouldn't want to wake up to a fresh bowl of oatmeal that's been cooking away peacefully overnight? It's a fantastic way for the whole family to start the day and gives you more time to do what you like without sacrificing on the quality or nutrition of your food.

Slow cookers are particularly useful for those of us who partake in a vegetarian or vegan diet. There is a common misconception that such diets are overly restrictive and limiting in protein, nutrients and flavor. But I believe this to be entirely wrong. In fact, I have 150 recipes listed for you that prove otherwise.

This collection of recipes provides both traditional and modern ideas for every meal of the day, whether you want a comforting and simple dish after a long day at work, or you would like to try something a little different, such as a slow cooker pizza recipe. Regardless of what you are in the mood for, I guarantee these recipes are packed full of natural ingredients and health benefits. I might have snuck the occasional treat recipe in as well.

Above all, this book will help you master slow cooking and give you the confidence to experiment and incorporate your own ideas. There are some recipes that require a little more preparation and effort when you're ready to try them. I promise the same principle of a delicious dish with minimal cleaning up will still remain.

Slow Cooking 101

It might look out of place on the kitchen counter because of its size, but our slow cooker always has a proud, prominent spot. Use a slow cooker effectively and it can be an incredible culinary tool that will reward you with fantastic flavors and some serious brownie points from friends and family.

Preparing the ingredients is the only real effort in slow cooking, but there are plenty of tips and tricks to help you get the most out of your time.

If you're new to slow cooking, then the 101 section will give you a good deal of knowledge about how to get the most out of these recipes. Follow these guidelines when using your slow cooker and you'll be rewarded with incredibly tasty and nourishing dishes that your body and mind will thank you for when the timer goes off.

The Basics

Make suitable space

Slow cookers are a safe way to cook food but do generate heat, so following a few simple guidelines never hurts. To begin, place the cooker a few inches from walls and away from your refrigerator and other appliances. It needs space or you'll be letting any heat dissipate. You may want to give it a permanent home; finding a good spot for your cooker means you won't neglect it or have to dig it out of a cupboard every time you want to use it.

Understand the settings

You'd be forgiven for thinking that the "high" heat setting cooks your food at a much hotter temperature than "low." In fact, the ultimate cooking temperature is the same on all the settings (around 210°F); the setting you choose just dictates how quickly the cooker reaches that temperature.

Look at your make and model

Naturally, different makes and manufacturers will result in slightly different cooking times and temperatures. If you are new to slow cooking or have invested in a new model, then base the cooking time on the general rule of when the vegetables are tender, it's cooked!

It is also worth keeping in mind that two hours of cooking on the low setting is the rough equivalent of cooking for one hour on high.

Know your cooker's limits and fill appropriately

You might be tempted to make a huge batch of your favorite soup or casserole, but you shouldn't overfill your slow cooker. It is recommended that you leave a two-inch gap between the food and the top of the cooker.

It is also worthwhile to layer ingredients in a way that suits their cooking time — root vegetables take longer to cook and hold up better than spinach, so they should be place on the bottom of the ceramic bowl, giving them maximum heat exposure.

Match the servings to the cooker

The majority of the recipes are based on a 4 to 6 quart cooker size. Bear in mind if you have a small cooker, then you will need to alter the amount of ingredients accordingly so it isn't overfilled. If you are using a recipe that serves 4 and you are cooking for only 2 people, then you can lower the quantities or store the leftovers.

Base cooking around your schedule

By taking your own daily schedule into account, you can make slow cooking an absolute breeze — from preparing oatmeal the night before so it's ready to eat first thing in the morning, to setting aside ingredients so they can be thrown into the cooker before you leave for work. Slow cooking is already very simple and easy, but the right preparation means you don't even have to think twice about creating a delicious curry that can last you several days.

Make sure the lid is on correctly

For a slow cooker to heat food effectively, a constant temperature of around 210°F is usually required. To achieve this temp, the lid must fit on snug. General wear and tear can dent and damage lids, resulting in heat escaping and ineffective cooking. So be sure to secure the lid correctly and take extra care of your cooker.

Cooking Tips

Stir sparingly and keep the lid on

Slow cooking usually requires very little attention, so only stir ingredients when a recipe advises it and avoid opening the lid unnecessarily as this allows heat to escape and can slow down cooking times. As you become more familiar with your slow cooker, you'll recognize how well it heats and if it has uneven heating areas. If this is the case, then stirring can actually help ensure thoroughly cooked ingredients.

Don't be tempted to add extra liquid

You might think a recipe either looks like it's going to be dry or needs more liquid, but remember that slow cooking retains a lot of moisture and vegetables have very high water content!

Follow tips when baking

Baking in a slow cooker can be extremely rewarding, but it can also be tricky. Make sure you use baking tins or trays that comfortably fit into your slow cooker, and grease them before adding ingredients. It can also be a good idea to rotate the tin halfway through baking as this ensures even cooking.

Be careful using kitchen or paper towels

Certain recipes (especially when baking) suggest you line the lid of the slow cooker with a clean kitchen towel or paper towel. Doing this can prevent condensation from forming on the cooker lid and dripping onto the mixture. It is important to ensure the towel does not touch the mixture and the lid is firmly on. You should also take care to keep the towels off the hot ceramic.

Season after, not before

It can be tempting to add seasoning at the start of cooking, and while some recipes allow for this, slow cookers do tend to mellow these flavors, making it more worthwhile to season at the end of cooking instead. The same principle applies for fresh herbs, as they have a tendency to break up and blacken if cooked for too long.

Then just wait...

These are all simple tips to take into account when cooking, and the majority of them will become second nature to you. So once you have prepared the ingredients and added them the slow cooker, all you really have left to do is walk away and not think about it for a few hours until the food is ready to serve.

Breakfast Recipes

Lazy Slow-Cooked Oatmeal

Porridge is an ideal way to start the day, providing the whole family with lots of fiber and slow-release energy from complex carbohydrates. But if you find mornings too hectic to make it from scratch, my slow-cooked porridge recipe gives you creamy and delicious porridge that's ready as soon as you wake up. All you'll need to do is add your favorite delicious toppings.

Prep Time: 5 minutes
Cook Time: 7-8 hours
Serves 4

1 cup jumbo oats (you can experiment with a variety)
4 cups milk
Pinch of salt
Honey and apple, to serve
Sliced banana and cacao powder, to serve
Blueberries, almonds and a pinch of cinnamon powder, to serve

Method

Lightly grease the inside of the cooker if you are worried about the porridge sticking.

Add the first three ingredients into the slow cooker. Remember there are a variety of different oats and milks you can experiment with, but I recommend trying almond milk. Give the mixture a good stir to ensure there are no clumped oats and then cook on the slow cooker's lowest heat overnight (7-8 hours).

In the morning give your porridge a good stir and if required add a touch more milk to get your preferred consistency.

Then serve into bowls and add your favorite toppings. Why not try giving our serving suggestions a go!

Good-For-You Granola

Granola has become an incredibly popular choice for breakfasts, but it's often filled with additional sugar and can be quite costly. Fortunately, with your trusty slow cooker by your side, you can be in complete control of what goes into your granola and can customize it entirely to suit your personal tastes. Homemade granola offers many benefits, from aiding weight loss to regulating digestion, making it well worth trying. Here's my personal favorite recipe, but remember there's no right or wrong combination when it comes to making your own granola.

Prep Time: 5 minutes
Cook Time: 3-4 hours
Serves 4

4 cups oats
¼ cup dried coconut
¼ cup cranberries
¼ cup raisins
¼ cup pumpkin seeds
¼ cup chia seeds
¼ cup sliced or crushed almonds
¼ cup honey
2 tablespoons of coconut oil

Method

Add all the ingredients into the slow cooker, except the honey and coconut oil.

Melt the coconut oil and combine with the honey. Pour this mixture into the cooker and either use a wooden spoon or your hands to make everything evenly coated. Don't worry if any of the mixture is sticking together — it is granola after all!

Cook on high for 3-4 hours. Be sure to not tightly close the lid; leave some breathing space. Check the cooker regularly to ensure the mixture isn't burning and to stir.

Once cooked, allowed the granola to rest. Eat it with your choice of milk or yogurt.

Versatile Southern Grits

Don't be fooled by the name. Grits are anything but gritty! A creamy and delicious treat, it is a staple that is ideal for any time of day, but I especially enjoy it in the mornings. Whether eaten alone or with your favorite sweet or savory toppings, grits is a versatile meal that rivals oatmeal and is an ideal way to start the day.

Grits provide you with a healthy carbohydrate that is great for those with high cholesterol or diabetics thanks to its low glycemic response.

Prep Time: 15 minutes
Cook Time: 7-8 hours
Serves 3-4

1 cup of grits
5 cups of water
½ tablespoon of salt
3 tablespoons of butter
10 ounces grated cheddar cheese (optional for savory flavor)
To serve sweet:
Maple syrup
Banana
Mixed berries
Compote
To serve savory:
Scallions
Red pepper
Caramelized onion
Sautéed spinach
Tomatoes

Method

Grease the inside of your slow cooker and then add all the ingredients. Stir the mixture — the grits will naturally sit at the bottom. If you want to make savory grits, then once the cooker has heated up, slowly stir in the cheese until it has melted. Cover and cook on the lowest temperature for 7-8 hours. This is ideally done overnight. When it comes to serving the grits, feel free to experiment with a variety of fresh toppings, starting with my suggestions.

Healthy Wheat Berry Salad with Fruit & Nuts

It's likely you aren't too familiar with wheat berries; they are in fact the whole wheat grain. This means they are packed with all their nutrients, protein and vitamins, making them a fantastic addition to your diet. By slow cooking the wheat, you create a chewy texture that perfectly complements the crispness of the sliced fruit.

Prep Time: 20 minutes
Cook Time: 3 hours
Serves 2

Salad:
2 cups cooked wheat berries
4 cups water
1 orange
¼ cup dried cranberries
¼ cup raisins
1 apple, diced
½ cup chopped pecans

Dressing:
1 tablespoon honey
1 tablespoon coconut oil

Method

To cook the wheat berries, place them in the slow cooker with the water and cook on high for 3 hours or until they are chewy. Once cooked, the wheat berries keep up to a month, so this process doesn't have to be repeated.

Finely grate the zest from the orange into a large serving bowl. Juice the orange into a small separate bowl and toss in the cranberries and raisins. Let the mixture sit at room temperature for 20 minutes. Mix the cooked wheat berries, diced apple, and pecans in with the orange zest.

To create the dressing, mix the orange juice with the honey and coconut oil, and then pour over the combined ingredients, and serve.

The Easy Breakfast Omelet

Omelets are an ideal way to start the day. They are incredibly versatile and can work with practically anything in them.

Eggs are a source of quality protein and good cholesterol, and have been proven to satisfy appetites, helping to keep you fuller for longer. This makes them a go-to food for anyone who usually snacks before lunch.

Prep Time: 5-10 minutes
Cook Time: 2 hours
Serves 4

Omelet:
6 eggs
Salt and pepper
1 garlic clove, minced
½ onion, sliced
1 handful broccoli florets
1 red bell pepper, sliced

Garnish:
Grated cheese (optional)
3 tomatoes, chopped
Fresh parsley

Method

Grease the inside of the slow cooker to avoid sticking.

Whisk the eggs in a bowl, adding seasoning and the minced garlic clove.

Put the vegetables in the cooker and cover with the egg mixture. Stir the contents until evenly coated and then cook on high for 2 hours. Check the omelet after the 1½ hours.

When the eggs are set, the omelet is ready. If you'd like to add cheese, then sprinkle it on top of the omelet and allow to melt.

Cut the omelet into slices and serve with the tomatoes and parsley as garnish.

Apple and Date Crunch Power Snack

A perfect snack or even dessert, this recipe can be packed with your favorite healthy snacks, from nuts and seeds to dried fruits. Dates are an ideal addition to any diet as they contain an impressive level of iron, making them perfect for vegetarians or vegans who need to boost their iron levels.

Prep Time: 10 minutes
Cook Time: 3 hours
Serves 4-5

6 small apples, cored and quartered
1 cup dates, chopped
1 cup pecan pieces
1 cup dried cherries or other dried fruit you like
1 teaspoon cinnamon
¼ cup coconut oil, melted
¼ cup agave nectar or other natural sweetener
½ cup filtered water

Method

Add the apples, dates, pecans and dried cherries to the slow cooker. Sprinkle with cinnamon, and mix.

Warm the coconut oil and agave in a small pan over a low heat. Pour over the apple mixture and add the water. Cover and cook for 3 hours on high.

The Paleo Breakfast Casserole

Slow cookers are renowned for stews and casseroles, which are usually associated with hearty dinners. This recipe takes the casserole principle and gives it a breakfast twist. It's a great way to start the day and can be made in advance and stored throughout the week to ensure every day starts the right way.

Prep Time: 10 minutes
Cook Time: 8-10 hours
Serves 4

Quorn sausages, coarsely chopped
1 small onion, diced
10 eggs (or egg replacer)
1 cup coconut milk
1 small butternut squash, diced

Method

Brown the sausages in a frying pan. Add the onion and cook until it softens.

Whisk the eggs (or replacement) with the coconut milk. Grease the slow cooker.

Add the squash, then the sausage and onion mixture, and finally the eggs to the slow cooker. Cover and cook on low for 8-10 hours, preferably overnight.

Thick & Creamy Homemade Yogurt

When life gives you a slow cooker...make yogurt! That's right, your slow cooker can even make yogurt as well.

This recipe is a simple one but results in creamy, coconutty and delicious yogurt. The benefit of making it yourself is that you only have to use 3 ingredients and you end up with a sugar- and dairy-free breakfast or snack.

Prep Time: 10 minutes
Cook Time: 2½ hours
Serves 6

1 gallon coconut milk
1 cup coconut milk yogurt
2 teaspoons agar-agar flakes

Method

Pour the milk into the slow cooker. Cover and cook on high for 2½ hours.

Turn off the slow cooker and allow the mixture to cool for 3 hours.

Mix together the yogurt and agar-agar flakes. When the milk has cooled, add the mixture to it and stir well. Put the lid back on, cover the cooker in a thick towel and let it sit for 8 hours.

Remove the lid and either strain any excess liquid or mix in. Chill in the fridge and serve with fresh fruit.

Hearty Hash Brown Casserole

A hearty and healthy breakfast is an ideal way to start the day. By arranging this hash brown recipe the night before, you're setting yourself up for a morning with no fuss.

This breakfast casserole contains plenty of vegetables, nutrients and carbohydrates from the potatoes that will help keep you going until lunch.

Prep Time: 10 minutes
Cook Time: 8 hours
Serves 6

6 slices of vegetarian bacon
30 ounces frozen shredded hash browns, thawed
Salt and pepper, to taste
1 onion, diced
1 green bell pepper, chopped
1 red bell pepper, chopped
12 eggs (or egg replacer)
1 cup coconut milk
1 teaspoon dill
1 teaspoon garlic, minced

Method

Grease the inside of the slow cooker.

Brown the bacon in a frying pan and then cut into small pieces.

In a large bowl, add the potatoes, salt and pepper, and other vegetables. Then alternate layers of the potato mixture and bacon in the slow cooker.

Mix the eggs, milk, dill and garlic. Then pour over the ingredients in the cooker.

Cook on low for 8 hours.

Overnight Maple & Brown Sugar Oatmeal

More indulgent than your usual oatmeal, this maple and brown sugar recipe is ideal when you want to treat the kids or just need an extra boost in the morning. Steel-cut oats hold perfectly with the slow cooking, and you end with a beautiful sweetness and a satisfying bite.

Prep Time: 5-10 minutes
Cook Time: 7-8 hours
Serves 4-6

1½ cups almond milk or 6 cups water
2 cups steel-cut oats
¼ cup pure maple syrup
¼ cup packed light brown sugar
1 teaspoon ground cinnamon
¾ cup dried blueberries (optional)
½ teaspoon salt

Method

Combine all of the ingredients in the slow cooker, and mix well.

Cook for 7-8 hours (overnight is ideal) on low.

Stir again before serving.

Strawberry and Blueberry Oat Smash

Another variation on the traditional oatmeal recipe. This is so easy to make and is a healthy way to add additional color and flavor into your breakfast. The recipe is so delicious you might even mistake the flavor for strawberry ice cream!

Prep Time: 2 minutes
Cook Time: 7-8 hours
Serves 4-6

12 strawberries
1 handful of blueberries
2 cups rolled oats
1½ cups almond milk
¼ teaspoon vanilla extract
Yogurt, for serving
1 tablespoon strawberry jam, for serving

Method

Chop the strawberries into your preferred size. Add all the ingredients except the jam to the slow cooker, and cook on low for 7-8 hours.

Serve with a spoonful of yogurt and jam.

Once-a-Week PBJ Oatmeal

A variation of the classic oatmeal breakfast, this recipe has all the benefits of regular oatmeal but a little more indulgence. It's best to keep this as an occasional treat or control the levels of jam if it does become a weekly habit. Use any type of jam or nut butter you like. I recommend almond or cashew.

Prep Time: 5 minutes
Cook Time: 7-8 hours
Serves 2-3

½ cup steel-cut oats
2 cups almond milk (unsweetened)
3 tablespoons natural almond butter
3 tablespoons strawberry jam

Method

This oatmeal is best prepared the night before eating. Add the oats and milk to the slow cooker, and cook for 7-8 hours on low.

In the morning, stir the oatmeal well and then mix in the almond butter and jam.

Serve immediately.

Crispy and Chewy French Toast Casserole

Another simple recipe that is ideal as either a sweet breakfast or a dessert, this is a casserole version of French toast and is as easy to make as it is tasty. Either real eggs or egg replacer can be used to create this dish, depending on your preference.

Prep Time: 2-3 hours
Cook Time: 6 hours, 30 minutes
Serves 4-6

Casserole:
3½ cups almond milk
3 eggs
½ cup sugar
1 tablespoon vanilla essence
1 teaspoon cinnamon
½ teaspoon nutmeg
¼ teaspoon salt
1 loaf cinnamon bread, cut into 1-inch cubes

Topping:
½ cup toasted pecans, chopped
2 tablespoons butter
2 tablespoons flour
2 tablespoons brown sugar

Method

Whisk all the casserole ingredients except the bread in a large bowl. Add the bread to the mixture and combine. Refrigerate for several hours.

Grease the slow cooker to avoid sticking. Add the bread mixture to the slow cooker and cook on low for 6 hours.

Mix the topping ingredients together and sprinkle over the French toast. Cook for a further 30 minutes uncovered, and serve.

Simple Slow Cooker Blueberry Pancakes

Blueberry pancakes are a great way to start the day, giving your metabolism a jump-start with carbohydrates and your skin and brain a boost thanks to the antioxidants and phenols in blueberries. Did I mention that they also taste great and kids love them!

Prep Time: 15 minutes
Cook Time: 4 hours
Serves 3-4

1 cup almond milk
1 egg (or egg replacer)
2 tablespoons butter, melted
1 cup flour
2 teaspoons baking powder
1 tablespoon sugar
¾ cup blueberries

Prep Time
15 minutes

Cook Time
1 hour

Method

In a large bowl, combine and whisk the milk, egg and melted butter.

In another bowl, mix the flour, baking powder and sugar. Slowly combine the wet and dry ingredients.

Grease the slow cooker to prevent sticking. Pour half of the pancake mixture to cover the base of the cooker and add blueberries. Pour the remaining batter on top of the berries.

Cover and cook on high for 1 hour. Times may vary, so do a toothpick test to see if the pancake is cooked.

Serve with your choice of toppings, from fresh fruit and yogurt to maple syrup.

Lemony Raspberry Cheesecake Oatmeal

Don't let the name fool you! This oatmeal is another incredibly simple and tasty treat that works well as a breakfast, snack or dessert. In fact, the idea is for this oatmeal to be more of a dessert, hence the cheesecake.

It's a creamy, sweet and tangy combination and a pretty healthy dessert if I do say so myself.

Prep Time: 5 minutes
Cook Time: 7-8 hours
Serves 2-4

½ cup steel-cut oats
2 cups coconut milk
1 teaspoon lemon extract
½ teaspoon vanilla extract
Sweetener if desired
Raspberry Greek or dairy-free yogurt, for serving

Method

Place all the ingredients except the sweetener and yogurt into the slow cooker and leave overnight for 7-8 hours.

Once cooked, stir the oatmeal and serve with a generous amount of yogurt.

Bread recipes

Grandma's Cornbread

Cornbread is a great addition to lunchtimes and dinner. Even though it's moist and easy to make, this staple bread also has some surprising benefits because of cornmeal, which is a whole grain. Whole grains contain the bran as well as the germ and endosperm of the grain — meaning they still have all of the nutrients. So you get plenty of fiber per serving, which helps to control blood sugar and cholesterol.

Prep Time: 10 minutes
Cook Time: 2 hours
Serves 8

1 tablespoon unsalted butter (or oil)
1½ cups cornmeal
1½ cups all-purpose flour
2 tablespoons sugar
1 tablespoon baking powder
1 teaspoon kosher salt
1 teaspoon chili powder (optional)
2 cups buttermilk (or non-dairy alternative)
2 large eggs (or egg replacer)

Method

Melt the butter in the slow cooker on high heat. Spread it around the cooker or use oil instead of butter.

Mix the cornmeal, flour, sugar, baking powder, salt and chili powder in a bowl. Stir in the milk and eggs (or their replacements).

Pour in the cornbread mixture and cover. Cook on high for 2 hours.

Allow it to cool and serve.

The Perfect Pumpkin Bread

This pumpkin bread is wonderfully moist and slightly spiced, providing an incredibly lovely taste with each bite. It's also a great way to make use of any leftover pumpkin or if you have canned pumpkin in your pantry and no recipe to match. And it's perfect as a mid-day snack and can be customized to your liking with orange zest or vanilla.

Prep Time: 15 minutes
Cook Time: 2½-3 hours
Serves 1 loaf

1½ cups sugar
½ cup vegetable oil
2 medium eggs (or egg replacer)
1 can (16 ounce) solid pack pumpkin
1½ cups all-purpose flour
1 teaspoon cinnamon
1 teaspoon nutmeg
1 teaspoon baking soda
½ teaspoon baking powder
½ teaspoon salt

Method

Use a slow cooker that is large enough to fit your loaf pan (preferably 9x5x3 inch). Stabilize the pan with aluminum foil if necessary. Coat the pan with non-stick spray or grease.

Add the sugar and oil in a large bowl. Mix in the eggs and pumpkin.

Combine the dry ingredients in a separate bowl. Then add the dry and wet mixtures, stir thoroughly and add to the slow cooker.

Cover the top of the cooker with a kitchen towel to prevent condensation, and cook on high for 2½-3 hours. Test the center with a knife, and if it comes out cleanly, then it's cooked.

Bananas About Banana Bread

Let the slow cooker do all the work and bake this sumptuous and sweet cake-like bread. An ideal solution for overripe bananas, this bread doesn't have to be an overly sugary treat. In fact, the addition of mashed bananas provides a good deal of potassium, which helps lower blood sugar and amino acids that can help boost your mood. Making it perfect for those rainier days.

Prep Time: 15 minutes
Cook Time: 4 hours
Serves 1 loaf

2 eggs (or egg replacer)
1 cup sugar
½ cup butter, softened
1 teaspoon baking powder
½ teaspoon baking soda
½ teaspoon salt
3 medium ripe bananas, mashed
2 cups flour

Method

Thoroughly mix the eggs, sugar and butter in a bowl. Add the baking powder, soda and salt.

Add the bananas and flour, alternating the two until all the ingredients are combined.

Grease a bread pan and pour the mixture into it. Use a kitchen towel on the cooker to prevent condensation. Cook in the slow cooker for 4 hours on low. Let cool and serve.

Easy Artisan Rosemary Bread

There's no feeling like making your own bread, especially when the warm aromas of rosemary and olive oil take over your kitchen. This recipe is the perfect pairing for any of the soups or Irish stew. It's also pretty easy to make and it's vegan too!

Prep Time: 1.25 hours
Cook Time: 2 hours
Serves 1 loaf

1¼ cups warm water
2¼ teaspoons packet dry active yeast
1 teaspoon sugar
1 teaspoon sea salt, divided
¼ cup fresh rosemary, chopped, divided
3 tablespoons extra virgin olive oil, plus more for drizzling
3½ cups all-purpose flour

Method

Mix the water, yeast and sugar in a large bowl. Allow it to rest for 10 minutes.

Stir in some of the salt, half the rosemary, the olive oil, and all of the flour. Mix until completely combined.

Grease a large bowl, placing the dough in it. Cover and allow it to sit for 1 hour.

Remove the dough and roll it on a floured surface. While it sits, set the cooker to high and line it with parchment paper that is raised along the sides so you can easily remove the bread.

Place the dough in the cooker and cover with the remaining salt and rosemary. Cook for 2 hours. If you like your bread with a crust, then put it under the broiler for a few minutes until golden. Let cool and serve.

The Easy Classic White Loaf

A slow cooker offers a great deal of diversity, making it possible to create anything from exotic curries to poached figs, but it is also a dynamo at churning out regular dishes and sides too.

If you're fond of making your own bread, then this white bread recipe is a must try. This recipe is entirely from scratch, so you can control the exact ingredients and be rewarded with a great flavor and no hidden or unnecessary nasties.

Prep Time: 25 minutes
Cook Time: 2+ hours
Serves 1 loaf

2¼ teaspoons active dry yeast
¼ plus 1 cup lukewarm water
1 teaspoon plus ¼ cup sugar
1 egg (or egg replacer)
¼ cup vegetable oil
1 teaspoon salt
3 ½ to 4 cups all-purpose flour
1 tablespoon butter, melted

Instructions

Combine the yeast, ¼ cup of water, and 1 teaspoon of sugar. Allow the ingredients to naturally mix for 10 minutes.

In a different bowl, combine the egg, oil, 1 cup lukewarm water, sugar, salt and yeast mixture. Use an electric mixer to beat the contents for 2 minutes.

Add the flour to the mixture and continue beating with the electric mixer on low until the mixture firms up and becomes gummy. Once this happens, place the dough on a lightly floured surface and knead until the dough becomes elastic.

Line the cooker with parchment paper (note: do not pre-warm the cooker) and place the ball of dough in the center. Cover and cook on high for 2 hours. Use a kitchen towel under the cover to prevent condensation.

Cookers heat at different speeds, so check your loaf after 1½ hours and then every 15 minutes or so.

The crust won't brown, so don't use the color as an indication of doneness.

Once it's done, you can leave the bread as is if you like a soft crust. If you prefer a crusty loaf, then place the loaf under a broiler for a few minutes until golden.

Old-Fashioned Cinnamon Rolls

There really is nothing quite like the fragrance of warm homemade cinnamon rolls! And these have to be one of the easiest from-scratch rolls you'll ever likely make. In fact, chances are you'll already have most of the ingredients in your kitchen already, which begs the question...why haven't you made these fluffy gems sooner?

Prep Time: 25 minutes
Cook Time: 2 hours
Serves 10-12

Dough:
   1⅓ cups warm water
   1 tablespoon active dry yeast
   2 tablespoons honey
   3½ cups flour
   1 teaspoon salt

Filling:
   ½ cup sugar
   ¼ cup brown sugar
   1 tablespoon cinnamon
   4 tablespoons butter, completely softened

Frosting:
   2 tablespoons butter, softened
   2 ounces cream cheese, softened (or replacement)
   1 teaspoon vanilla
   3 cups powdered sugar
   2-3 tablespoons almond milk

Method

Dough:
Add the water, yeast and honey to a mixer bowl with a dough hook and combine. Let the mixture rest for 5 minutes. It will bubble and rise.

Add the flour and salt to the bowl. Turn the mixer to low and mix until all the ingredients come together. Mix at a slightly faster speed for a further 10 minutes, then move the dough to a floured surface.

Filling:
Whisk together the sugars and cinnamon.

After the dough has rested, roll it into a rectangle (roughly 9x15 inch) and use a pizza cutter or knife to create a perfectly straight rectangle. Run the dough with the butter and cover with the filling mixture. Tightly roll one length of the dough to the other, and then use a knife to cut into 10-12 equal pieces.

Line the cooker with parchment paper. Place the rolls face up in the cooker and use a kitchen towel under the lid of your slow cooker to prevent condensation. Cook the rolls on high for 1½-2 hours until they're no longer doughy. Once cooked, allow to cool.

Frosting:
Mix the butter and cream cheese together until fluffy. Gradually add the vanilla and sugar, mixing continuously. Then slowly add the almond milk until the frosting is smooth and pourable. Drizzle over the cinnamon rolls to serve.

Fresh and Soft Vegan Pizza Rolls

Slow cookers wouldn't seem to lend themselves to making good pizza, but this pizza roll recipe — which can easily be made vegan by replacing the egg — is a simple way to make a tasty side for get-togethers and sharing.

Prep Time: 25 minutes
Cook Time: 1 hour, 50 minutes
Serves 8

2¼ teaspoons active dry yeast
½ cup warm water
½ cup nondairy milk
2 tablespoons coconut oil
2 teaspoons sugar
1 teaspoon sea salt
Egg substitute or 1 egg
3 cups all-purpose flour
½ cup pizza sauce

Method

In a small bowl, add the yeast to the warm water and stir. Set the bowl to one side.

Using a mixer with a paddle attachment, combine the milk, coconut oil, sugar, salt and egg substitute (or egg).

Stir on a low speed and pour in the yeast mixture, mix until fully combined.

Equip a dough hook attachment if possible, and mix in the flour for 6 minutes. You can expect the dough to be a little sticky, but if you find it too hard to work with, add a little more flour.

Cut the ball of dough into 10-12 pieces and roll into balls.

Line the slow cooker with parchment paper.

Put some of the pizza sauce in a bowl and roll each of the dough balls in it. Then place them on the parchment paper in the cooker.

There will be gaps in the dough — this is fine but be careful not to overfill or press the dough too close to the sides.

Cover and cook on low for 1 hour. Then turn the cooker to high and cook for 30 minutes. Brush the remainder of the sauce on top of the dough and cook for a further 20 minutes.

Once done, rest on a wire rack and serve either hot or cold.

Appetizer Recipes

Easy Marinated Artichoke Hearts

As well as creating wonderful stews and soups, the slow cooker is also capable of making a good number of appetizers that you probably thought weren't possible. Marinated artichoke hearts are the perfect example. By using a slow cooker, the gentle heat infuses lots of complex and deep flavors into the artichokes. You're also getting all of the goodness of the artichokes, from their incredibly high levels of antioxidants and dietary fiber.

Prep Time: 10 minutes
Cook Time: 1-2 hours
Serves 6

18 ounces frozen artichoke hearts, thawed, patted dry, and
    halved
1 cup extra-virgin olive oil
½ cup pitted Kalamata olives, halved
¾ teaspoon grated lemon zest
2 tablespoons juice
3 peeled garlic cloves, crushed
2 sprigs fresh thyme
1 teaspoon salt
¼ teaspoon red pepper flakes
1 block feta cheese, cubed (optional or alternative)

Method

Combine the artichoke hearts with all the ingredients except the cheese and cook on low for 1 to 2 hours.

Remove the thyme, add the feta to the cooker, and gently stir. Allow it to heat for 5 minutes, then serve.

Tantalizing Eggplant Caponata

Caponata is a vibrant and fun mix of vegetables, but in this recipe we are focusing on eggplant. Eggplants offer a unique range of health benefits, from helping to manage diabetes to reducing stress, which we could all benefit from.

This slow cooker recipe is an effortless one, utilizing spices and sweetness to make a flavorful caponata spread.

Prep Time: 5 minutes
Cook Time: 7-8 hours
Serves 6-8

4 eggplants, cut into small cubes
1 small onion, chopped finely
3 tablespoons raisins
3 tablespoons olive oil
3 tablespoons balsamic vinegar
2 tablespoons pine nuts
2 tablespoons brown sugar
2 tablespoons lemon juice, fresh
½ teaspoon cumin powder
¼ teaspoon harissa paste
¼ teaspoon cinnamon

Method

Add all the ingredients to the slow cooker and turn the heat to low. Cook for 7-8 hours, checking occasionally and stirring. The eggplant should be very soft and there should be little or no liquid in the cooker. If there is liquid, then turn the heat up to high and prop the lid open, cooking until it reduces.

Store in the fridge for up to a week.

Creamy White Bean and Garlic Hummus

A creamy and tasty homemade hummus that is perfect when served with fresh veggies, crisps or toasted pita bread. Not only is hummus a fantastic snack but the benefits of white bean hummus are plentiful as well, helping to control weight and reduce blood sugar.

Prep Time: 10 minutes
Cook Time: 4 hours on high/8 hours on low
Serves 4

⅔ cup dried white beans, rinsed
6 garlic cloves, peeled
¼ cup extra virgin olive oil
Juice of 1 lemon
Salt and black pepper, to taste

Method

Place the beans and garlic in the slow cooker. Cover them with water, stopping about 2 inches above the beans. Cover and cook on low for 8 hours or high for 4 hours, until the beans are tender.

Drain the contents and transfer to a blender. Add the olive oil and lemon juice, blend until smooth, and season.

Golden Garlic Herb Mushrooms

This is one of the simplest and best ways to cook mushrooms. This dish provides mushrooms with the center stage to shine, and you'll find with very little prep, you'll be rewarded with a delicious and flavorful meal.

Another reward for making this dish: Like humans, mushrooms also produce vitamin D and you'll be getting a good dose of it to help protect against disease and strengthen your bones.

Prep Time: 5 minutes
Cook Time: 3-4 hours
Serves 4-6

24 ounces cremini mushrooms
4 cloves garlic, minced
2 bay leaves
1 cup vegetable broth
½ teaspoon dried basil
½ teaspoon dried oregano
¼ teaspoon dried thyme
2 tablespoons unsalted butter (or alternative)
2 tablespoons chopped fresh parsley leaves
Salt and freshly ground black pepper, to taste

Method

Add all the ingredients except the butter and parsley to the slow cooker (), stirring in the broth, and season.

Cover and cook on low for 3-4 hours, until the mushrooms are browned and tender.

Stir in the butter during the last 15 minutes of cooking. Garnish with parsley and salt and pepper, and serve.

Beer Cheese Fondue

Ideal as a party food or if you feel like treating yourself, this fondue recipe is super easy and will have you and your friends coming back for more.

Prep Time: 5 minutes
Cook Time: 2-4 hours
Serves 6-8

12 ounces beer
2 shallots, finely diced
1 garlic clove, minced
1 cup Gruyere cheese, grated
2 cups extra sharp cheddar cheese, grated
1 tablespoon cornstarch
1 teaspoon dry mustard
1/2 teaspoon nutmeg
Salt and pepper to taste

Method

Add all the ingredients except the salt and pepper into the slow cooker and mix. Cover and cook on low for 2-4 hours, stirring occasionally.

Add the salt and pepper to taste before serving. Serve with anything from chips to crusty bread. To make the fondue slightly healthier, serve with chopped veggies.

Fresh and Exciting Tomatillo Salsa Verde

This authentic Mexican salsa verde has a wonderful flavor. By cooking it, you're getting a sweet-sour richness that is the perfect complement to tortillas and refried beans.

Tomatillos contain all the right ingredients for optimal nutrition, providing 20% of your daily-recommended vitamin C, plenty of fiber and a healthy amount of iron.

Prep Time: 10 minutes
Cook Time: 3 hours
Serves 6

1 pound tomatillos, husked
½ cup onions, finely chopped
2 teaspoons garlic, minced
1 serrano chile pepper, minced
1-2 limes, juiced
½ teaspoon cumin
1 teaspoon salt
2 tablespoons chopped cilantro
1 tablespoon chopped fresh oregano

Method

Add the tomatillos, onions, garlic and pepper to the slow cooker. Pour in the lime juice, cumin, salt and boiling water.

Cover and cook on high for 1½ hours, then reduce to low for a further 1½ hours.

Add the cilantro and oregano. Use a blender to puree the mixture until smooth or your preferred texture.

Main Meal Recipes

Quinoa & Black Bean Stuffed Peppers

Quinoa has become one of the world's most popular health foods. High in all the important nutrients, including fiber, protein and magnesium, it is something you'll find in all vegetarian homes.

This stuffed pepper recipe is a great way to liven up quinoa and makes a nice change from having it as the base for a meal. Like any good slow cooker recipe, there is very little preparation involved for the amount of goodness you're getting. Serve with a fresh salad and avocado for even more health points.

Prep Time: 20 minutes
Cook Time: 3 hours
Serves 5

5 bell peppers
1 cup quinoa (rinsed if required)
½ cup black beans
1 can tomato sauce
2 carrots, diced
1 medium onion, diced
2 garlic cloves, minced
½ teaspoon smoker paprika
½ teaspoon cumin
1 cup cheddar cheese (or alternative), divided
Fresh cilantro (to garnish)

Method

Cut the tops off the peppers and remove the seeds and ribs.

In a bowl, combine the quinoa, beans, tomato sauce, carrots, onion, spices and ½ cup of cheese. Fill each pepper with the mixture.

Pour ½ cup of water into the cooker and then add the peppers. Cook on high for 3 hours. Toward the end of the cooking time, add the remaining cheese to the tops of the peppers and allow to melt.

Serve the peppers with the cilantro as a garnish.

Colorful & Flavorful Italian Vegetable Bake

This Italian bake is a great way of combining plenty of vegetables rich in fiber and nutrients. Eggplants provides a unique taste and texture and also serves as a great all-rounder when it comes to the number of vitamins and minerals they contain, from fiber to potassium and vitamin C.

This is a vibrant dish for slow cookers, layering the best of the seasonal ingredients available with bread to soak up all the juices. It's even better when eaten the next day.

Perfect as a main dish or served in smaller quantities as a side.

Prep Time: 15 minutes
Cook Time: 5-6 hours
Serves 6

1 can chopped tomatoes
½ teaspoon dried oregano or fresh oregano leaves
1 pinch chilli flakes
3 garlic cloves, minced
2 eggplants, sliced
2 zucchini, sliced
4-6 roasted red peppers, sliced
2 beef tomatoes, sliced
1 baguette, sliced into 1-centimeter pieces (optional)
2 mozzarella (or alternative), divided
Fresh basil

Method

Gently heat the canned tomatoes, seasoning and garlic in a pan.

Meanwhile, begin to layer the eggplant, zucchini, peppers and tomato slices, seasoning well. Pour over half the sauce, then layer in the baguette slices with half the mozzarella. Repeat this step once more, so you have another layer of the vegetables with tomato sauce topped by the bread and mozzarella. Then cook on high for 5-6 hours.

If you'd like a golden and crisp finish, then use your grill for several minutes before serving. Garnish with basil and serve immediately.

Sticky & Spicy Sweet Potato Chili

Sweet potato is the ideal ingredient in vegetable chili, providing a great contrast to the heat of the chilies. What can I say about sweet potatoes that hasn't been said before? They provide vegetarians and vegans with iron, which is vital in giving our bodies energy and supporting a healthy immune system.

They're also a slow-release sugar, preventing any blood sugar spikes as their natural sugars are slowly released. This makes sweet potato chili an ideal lunchtime meal to keep you at your best throughout the day. Chock-full of other hearty vegetables, this chili recipe is an essential addition to any slow cooker recipe book.

Feel free to spice it up even more with fresh chilies or chili powder.

Prep Time: 15 minutes
Cook Time: 4-5 hours
Serves 4-6

2 sweet potatoes, peeled and cut into 1½ inch chunks
1 cubed carrot
2 garlic cloves, minced
1 onion, sliced
1 red pepper, chopped
1 can tomatoes
1 can beans, drained and rinsed
1 teaspoon cocoa powder
1 tablespoon chili powder
1 teaspoon ground cumin
Salt and pepper
1 cup water

Method

Combine all the contents in the slow cooker, adding the 1 cup of water last.

Cover and cook for 4-5 hours, checking to see when the sweet potatoes are tender and the chili sauce has thickened. Decide when the chili is ready based upon how firm you like your sweet potato.

Serve the chilli with rice or tortilla chips and fresh greens.

Beautifully Fragrant Pumpkin and Chickpea Curry

Halloween often does pumpkins a disservice; they're often associated more with this one day of the year than as a vegetable with many health benefits.

Packed full of carotenoids that can keep cancer cells at bay and keep skin wrinkle free, they also provide over 200% of our daily vitamin A intake, helping us keep our vision clear.

If you are partial to a creamy and hearty curry, then this is the one for you. The vegan recipe is incredibly tasty for how simple it is to prepare — the only part that takes any concentration is cutting the pumpkin.

It is a perfect dinner to make on the slow cooker for all the family to enjoy.

Prep Time: 15-20 minutes
Cook Time: 3 hours
Serves 6

1 medium/large pumpkin
1 can chickpeas, drained and rinsed
1 can coconut milk
1 red pepper, chopped
½ onion, chopped
2 tablespoons red curry paste
2 teaspoons paprika
1 teaspoon ground cumin
Salt and pepper
1½ cups water
Fresh cilantro, for garnish

Method

Prepare the pumpkin by deseeding and cutting into 1-inch cubes. Take care removing the skin.

Add the pumpkin, chickpeas, coconut milk, red pepper, onion, paste, spices and water to the slow cooker. Cover and cook for 3-4 hours on low.

Check on the curry after a few hours, season to taste, and if you'd prefer a thicker consistency, then remove some of the liquid. It is also possible to remove some of the curry and blend it in a food processor, adding it back into the cooker for a smoother and thicker curry.

Serve with rice and garnish with fresh cilantro.

Curried Red Lentil Dal

An ideal comfort food, this red lentil dal is a hearty meal that is bursting with health benefits. Of all the legumes and nuts, lentils contain the third highest level of protein. They're also low in calories, containing virtually no fat — making them perfect for weight loss. The recipe itself comes packed full of flavor and can be made in bulk to last a few days or freeze for a later date.

Prep Time: 20 minutes
Cook Time: 4-5 hours on high, 8 hours on low
Serves 2-8

2 teaspoons cumin seeds
2 teaspoons mustard seeds
2 teaspoons onion seeds
3 cups red lentils, soaked and drained
6 cups water
1 can diced tomatoes
1 onion, diced
3 garlic cloves, minced
1 tablespoon grated ginger
1 tablespoon turmeric
½ teaspoon ground cardamom
1 teaspoon salt
1 bay leaf
Fresh cilantro, for garnish

Method

Toast the cumin, mustard and onion seeds in a pan for a few minutes until you begin to smell their aromas. Then set to the side.

Add the red lentils straight to the cooker and cover with the 6 cups of water. Follow with the tomatoes, onion, garlic, ginger, turmeric, cardamom, salt and bay leaf. Combine with the toasted seeds and cook either on high for 4-5 hours or on the low setting for 8 hours.

Check the lentils every once in a while, and if they aren't soft, then continue to cook them. You can also use these peeks as an opportunity to season the curry more if required.

When cooked, serve with brown rice and fresh cilantro.

Simple Black Bean and Spinach Enchiladas

Who said vegetarian meals have to be boring? Enchiladas are a surprisingly simple and filling meal for you to make with your slow cooker. The mashed black beans provide contrasting texture and a big dose of fiber, potassium and vitamin B6, all of which help to keep your body and heart healthy.

Enchiladas are another great opportunity to introduce your favorite vegetables to an easy-to-prepare meal. Team them with a green salad, some fresh pomegranate, and you'll have a meal bursting with flavor and color.

Prep Time: 20 minutes
Cook Time: 2-3 hours
Serves 4

1 can black beans, rinsed, divided
2 red peppers, sliced
1 bag spinach
1 can corn
2 cups grated cheese (or dairy-free alternative), divided
½ teaspoon ground cumin
1 red chili, sliced
1 pack small corn tortillas
2 jars salsa
3 scallions, sliced
Lime, sliced

Method

Mash half the beans in a bowl. Add the peppers, spinach, corn, 1 cup cheese, cumin and seasoning. Gently mix these contents together.

Use a spoon to evenly distribute the mixture onto the tortillas (decide how many you need based on the size of your cooker), and roll them up.

Pour 1 jar of the salsa into the slow cooker. Then place the tortillas into the cooker seam-side down and side by side. Top with the remaining sauce and cheese. Cook on low for 2-3 hours until the contents are heated through and the tortillas begin to get crispy. Serve immediately with guacamole, a fresh salad and a slice of lime.

5-a-Day Tagine

This tagine recipe is a hearty dish filled with nutritious root vegetables. A comforting meal that is also healthy, this "5-a-day" version gives you all your nutrients and vitamins packed into one convenient and tasty meal.

Don't be afraid to change things up a bit, from experimenting with leftovers or adding in your favorite vegetables.

It makes an ideal accompaniment to couscous, brown rice or with some crusty bread to soak up all the juices.

Prep Time: 15 minutes
Cook Time: 8 hours
Serves 4

4 carrots
3 parsnips
2 red onions, cut into wedges
2 red peppers, cut into chunks
1 large leek, chopped
3 garlic cloves, minced
5 dried apricots
1 teaspoon chilli powder
1 teaspoon paprika
1 teaspoon ground cumin
Salt and pepper, to taste
1 can chopped tomato
2 teaspoons honey

Method

Mix the vegetables and apricots together in the cooker. Season with the chilli powder, paprika, ground cumin, salt and pepper. Pour in the canned chopped tomato and honey, mixing the contents well.

Cover and cook for 8 hours on the low setting.

Full of Flavor Falafel

Falafel is a staple for a lot of vegetarians, being an ideal replacement for the likes of meatballs. As it mainly consists of chickpeas, you are eating a low calorie and high fiber meal that uses plenty of vegetables.

Have I forgotten to mention they taste amazing? Falafel is an ideal method of utilizing left over pulp from vegetable juices. Don't let all that goodness go to waste. Instead, make a spontaneous batch of falafel with it, as it'll often result in even more tender and flavorsome bite size pieces of heaven.

Prep Time: 15 minutes
Cook Time: 2-4 hours
Serves 2-8

1 can chickpeas, rinsed and drained
1 bunch Swiss chard, stemmed and cut
2 garlic cloves, minced
½ onion, finely chopped
1 teaspoon ground cumin
1 teaspoon ground cilantro
1 teaspoon salt
½ juiced lemon
½ cup bread crumbs
1 egg, whisked (not necessary but helps binding mixture)
Olive oil

Method

Add the chickpeas, Swiss chard, garlic, onion, spices and lemon juice to a food processor and blend. Gradually add the breadcrumbs if the mixture needs firming up or add the egg if the mixture needs help holding together. Alternatively you can use a little water to help bind it.

Shape golf-ball sized patties of the falafel.

Drizzle olive oil in the base of the slow cooker and add the falafels one at a time, coating both sides in oil. Cook on high for 2-4 hours. Cooking duration will vary depending on your slow cooker. Once the falafels are golden brown on both sides they're ready to serve.

Hearty Artichokes

Artichokes are often neglected because of their hard exteriors but provide greater antioxidant benefits per serving than many of the foods we traditionally consider the most anti-oxidant rich.

They also provide a nice variation to the usual soups and casseroles your slow cooker may be used to. Ideal as an elegant appetizer or center stage of the main course, this simple and tasty meal will expand your slow cooker's horizons.

Prep Time: 10 minutes
Cook Time: 3-4 hours
Serves 6

1 cup wholegrain breadcrumbs
1 clove garlic, minced
½ cup grated Parmesan cheese
1 handful chopped parsley
Salt and pepper
4-6 artichokes, tops removed and stems trimmed
Olive oil

Method

Combine the breadcrumbs, garlic, Parmesan, parsley, and salt and pepper in a bowl. Spread the artichoke leaves and fill the spaces with the mixture until all of it is used.

Place the artichokes in the cooker facing upwards. Drizzle olive oil generously over the artichokes.

Cover with the lid and cook on high for 3-4 hours. Check the leaves are tender before serving.

Spring Asparagus and Fennel Risotto

A simple and flavorful dish, this is a great alternative when you are looking to avoid potatoes or regular rice. Asparagus is a vegetable you should definitely be looking to include in your diet, since it's packed full of antioxidants and is one of the top fruits and vegetables that can neutralize cell-damaging free radicals.

Prep Time: 5-10 minutes
Cook Time: 2-3 hours
Serves 4

1 cup arborio rice, uncooked
1 bunch asparagus spears, chopped
1 teaspoon ground fennel
1 cup sliced mushrooms (optional)
1 bulb fennel, finely chopped
2 tablespoons finely chopped shallots
2 tablespoons minced garlic
2 cups vegetable stock
1 cup water
⅓ cup white wine
1 tablespoon lemon zest
½ cup Parmesan cheese (or similar alternative)
Salt and pepper, to taste

Method

Add all the ingredients except the lemon, cheese, and salt and pepper to the slow cooker. Cover and cook on low for 2-3 hours, or until the rice is to your liking.

Stir in the cheese and lemon, and season.

Simple Spinach and Cheese Frittata

Frittatas are very easy to make in the slow cooker, especially as the ingredients also tend to be ones that are often in our cupboards and fridges. Whether you're cooking this recipe for lunch or you want a savory breakfast, the frittata is a protein-filled meal that can be filled with all your favorite vegetables.

Prep Time: 10 minutes
Cook Time: 1-1½ hours
Serves 4-6

½ cup diced onion
1 cup mozzarella cheese, shredded (or alternative), divided
1 clove of garlic
5 eggs (or egg replacer)
2 tablespoons almond milk
1 cup spinach, chopped
1 roma tomato, diced
1 teaspoon extra virgin olive oil
Salt and pepper to taste

Method

In a frying pan, sauté the onion until it is tender. Whisk the onion, cheese and remaining ingredients, and add to the slow cooker.

Top with the remaining cheese. Cook on low for 1-1½ hours or until the eggs have set.

The Best Green Bean Casserole

This green bean casserole is a healthy and hearty meal, ideal for either lunch or dinner. The beans pack a nutritional punch, helping your body fight free radicals and giving you a good dose of fiber, iron, calcium and magnesium. Best served with brown rice or a thick slice of crusty bread.

Prep Time: 20 minutes
Cook Time: 2½-3½ hours
Serves 4-6

2 slices vegan bacon, chopped finely
1 medium shallot, minced
2 cloves garlic, minced
¼ cup flour
2½ cups vegetarian broth
½ teaspoon salt
¼ teaspoon seasoning blend
¼ teaspoon pepper
1 can coconut cream
2 (12 ounce) bags frozen extra fine green beans or fresh (cook for less time)
1 cup Parmesan cheese (optional)
1 onion, chopped and fried

Method

Fry the bacon and shallot in a pan until brown. Add the garlic and cook for another minute. Add the flour to the pan and stir to coat the ingredients. Slowly add the broth and stir until smooth. Cook for several minutes until the sauce thickens. Add the seasoning and coconut cream, simmering for 2-4 minutes.

Add the frozen greens to the slow cooker and cover with the sauce.

Cover with the cheese (optional) and cook on high for 2½ to 3½ hours. Sprinkle with the onions in the last 15 minutes of cooking, then serve.

Indulgent Butternut Risotto

If you're after a luxurious meal, then look no further than this risotto. Combining the wonderful texture of arborio rice with sweet and creamy butternut squash, you'll feel as though you're being naughty but it's all good for you! Plus, it's an easy recipe to make, so there's no excuse not to try it. This recipe also utilizes my whole roasted squash recipe.

Prep Time: 10 minutes
Cook Time: 2-3 hours
Serves 4

1¼ cups arborio rice
2 tablespoons olive oil
4 cups vegetable broth
1 small onion, chopped
2 cloves garlic, chopped
1 teaspoon dried rubbed sage
1 teaspoon salt
¼ teaspoon pepper
1 butternut squash (cooked in advance), skinned and gently mashed
3 tablespoons Parmesan cheese (or alternative)
2 tablespoons butter (or dairy-free alternative)

Method

Mix the rice and olive oil in the slow cooker. Add all the ingredients except the squash, cheese and butter. Stir and cover. Cook on high for 2-3 hours.

Toward the end of cooking, add in the squash (as much as you see fit), cheese and butter. Stir to combine.

Serve immediately.

Stuffed Portobello Mushrooms

These stuffed mushrooms are guaranteed to be the juiciest and most flavorful you've ever had. Slow cooking them helps intensify their flavor, creating amazing results. Not to mention the fact that they're also packed full of antioxidants and so easy to make.

This recipe can be used as either an appetizer or as a main dish when teamed with rice and a salad.

Prep Time: 5-10 minutes
Cook Time: 3 hours
Serves 3

3 large Portobello mushrooms
1 garlic clove, minced
3 tablespoons parsley, chopped finely
1½ teaspoons lemon zest
⅛ teaspoon chili powder
1 large handful kefalotyri cheese (or dairy-free alternative)

Method

Clean the mushrooms and dry completely. Cut off the stalks and place upside down on aluminum foil squares.

Mix the other ingredients except the cheese in a small bowl. Spread this mixture over the insides of the mushrooms and sprinkle with the cheese. Lift the corners of the foil and pinch together on top to create closed tent-like tops.

Place in the cooker and heat on high for 3 hours (or until the mushrooms are completely cooked and the cheese has melted).

Provençal Ratatouille

This traditional stewed French vegetable dish makes for a super-healthy and hearty meal for either lunch or dinner.

If there's one thing I've learned about ratatouille, it is that exact proportions aren't too important!

Ratatouille uses anything and everything you like, so bring on all the seasonal vegetables that you'd love to try and include it in this dish.

Ratatouille works great on its own as a pasta sauce, in an omelet, on top of rice or as antipasti.

Prep Time: 10-15 minutes
Cook Time: 3 hours, 15 minutes
Serves 6+

2 red onions, chopped
3 Yukon Gold potatoes, chopped
3 large garlic cloves, peeled and smashed
¼ cup olive oil
3 medium tomatoes, seeded, cut into medium chunks
4 bell peppers, seeded and cut into large chunks
4 portobello mushroom caps, stems removed, cut into large chunks
2 small eggplant, cut into large chunks
3 small zucchini, cut into large chunks
¼ cup white wine
2 tablespoons fresh thyme leaves
3 tablespoons balsamic vinegar, or more to taste
2 tablespoons cornstarch
6 tablespoons water
Salt and fresh black pepper, to taste

Method

In a large frying pan, sauté the onions, potatoes and garlic with oil.

Cook until the onions become translucent and then transfer the contents to the slow cooker.

Add the remaining vegetables, wine and thyme, and cook on low for 3 hours.

Turn the cooker to high and add the balsamic, and season.

Mix the cornstarch with 6 tablespoons of water, then pour it into the slow cooker and stir. Cover and cook for 15 minutes.

Serve then and there, at room temperature, or chilled from the fridge.

Clean Spaghetti Squash & Pesto

If you love pasta but are conscious of carbs, then spaghetti squash is a natural and tasty alternative. It's a dish that is easy to make and everyone is guaranteed to enjoy it. The squash itself has many benefits as it contains a wide range of vitamins, including vitamins A, B-6, C and K. Let's face it, getting your vitamins this way is a lot more enjoyable than taking supplements!

Prep Time: 5 minutes
Cook Time: 4 hours
Serves 2

1 spaghetti squash
½ cup water
½ cup pesto sauce, more to taste
Salt and pepper

Method

Wash and dry the squash. Cut in half and scoop out the seeds.

Place the squash in the slow cooker, pouring the water around it. Cook on low for 4 hours.

Once cooked, remove from cooker and use a fork to scrape contents into a bowl. This will create the noodle effect.

Add the pesto and season. Serve right away or refrigerate.

Homemade Spaghetti Marinara

Often we resort to store-bought pasta sauces because we assume they're faster and tastier. But making your own marinara is not only simple to do — it tastes a whole lot better! The best news is that you have most of these ingredients in your kitchen already, so simply follow the below steps to pasta heaven.

Prep Time: 20 minutes
Cook Time: 8.5 hours
Serves 12

3 tablespoons extra-virgin olive oil
3 cups chopped onion
¼ cup minced garlic
½ cup diced celery
¼ teaspoon crushed red pepper
3 tablespoons chopped fresh oregano
¾ cup diced carrot
2 tablespoons unsalted tomato paste
½ cup dry red wine
5½ pounds plum tomatoes, peeled and chopped
¾ cup chopped fresh basil
Salt and black pepper

Method

Heat a frying pan over medium-high heat. Add the oil, onion, garlic, celery, red pepper, oregano and carrot, and sauté for 6-8 minutes. Add in the tomato paste and cook for a further 2 minutes, then the wine for 2 more minutes.

Transfer all the ingredients from the pan to the slow cooker and add the tomatoes. Cook on low for 8 hours.

Use an electric blender to blend and smooth the sauce. Add the basil and season, cook on high for a further 30 minutes.

Fantastic Veggie Lasagna

Veggie lasagna is one of those comforting dishes that we all know and love. By using your slow cooker you can master the art of creating delicious lasagna without having to worry about any of the usual issues. For this particular recipe, I love to blend the vegetable mixture slightly to create a wonderful and smooth texture. Once you've given it a go, it'll no doubt become a staple of your recipes. This recipe does use cheese, but feel free to experiment with a variety of dairy-free alternatives until you find the perfect combination.

Prep Time: 15-20 minutes
Cook Time: 4 hours
Serves 6

2 cups zucchini, broccoli, cauliflower, mushrooms and/or spinach
1 tablespoon dried Italian herbs
½ teaspoon garlic powder
1 teaspoon salt
1 large egg (or egg replacer)
1 (15 ounce) container ricotta cheese (or alternative)
½ cup Parmesan cheese, grated (or alternative)
1 (25 ounce) jar pasta sauce, divided
1 box lasagna noodles (uncooked)
2 cups mozzarella cheese, grated (or alternative)

Method

Add the vegetables to a food processer and pulse until roughly chopped.

Combine the herbs, garlic powder, salt, egg, ricotta and Parmesan in a bowl, stirring to combine.

Add half the pasta sauce to the slow cooker. Place a layer of the noodles on top of the sauce (break the noodles to fit if necessary).

Layer the cheese mixture on top and then top with a layer of the vegetables and some of the mozzarella. Repeat this step once more. Ensure the top of the dish has a later of noodles on top and pour over the remaining pasta sauce. Cover with grated cheese and cook on low for 4 hours.

Meat-free Lentil Shepherd's Pie

This lentil shepherd's pie is an amazing dish because of its simplicity and the nourishment you get from the lentils and sweet potato. You can use white or sweet potato, but I prefer the contrast of sweetness, so I tend to opt for the latter. It also adds vibrancy to the dish that the kids love.

Prep Time: 20-25 minutes (including mash potatoes)
Cook Time: 6 hours
Serves 6

1 large yellow onion, diced
2 large carrots, peeled and diced
4 stalks celery, diced
2 cloves garlic, crushed
1 tablespoon extra virgin olive oil
½ teaspoon freshly cracked black pepper
½ teaspoon dried thyme
1½ cups puy lentils, rinsed well
1 can (14 ounces) diced tomatoes
2 cups vegetable broth
1 cup frozen peas
4 cups mashed potatoes, or mashed sweet potatoes

Method

Add the onion, oil, carrot, celery, garlic, pepper, thyme, lentils and tomatoes in the cooker, covering in the vegetable broth. Cook on low for 6 hours.

20 minutes before the end of the cooking time, start to make mashed sweet potato. Add the peas at the end of the cooking time. Then either spread the mashed potatoes over the lentil mixture or add it individually on top of the served lentils.

For a crispier finish, add the lentils to ramekins or an ovenproof dish and top with the potato. Bake in the oven for 20-30 minutes until the potatoes brown.

Supreme Squash & Spinach Lasagna

A convenient and tasty lasagna recipe when you're short on ingredients and time, this recipe is ideal if you've taken my advice and roasted a squash or two at the start of the week! All you have to do then is layer the ingredients, pop the cooker on and come back to it when you're ready to serve.

Prep Time: 15 minutes
Cook Time: 3-4 hours
Serves 6

2 (10 ounce) packets winter squash puree (or homemade pureed squash)
⅛ teaspoon ground nutmeg
1 (32 ounce) packet ricotta
6 cups baby spinach
Salt and pepper, to taste
Lasagna noodles
2 cups grated mozzarella

Method

Mix the squash and nutmeg in a medium bowl.

In another bowl, combine the ricotta, spinach, and salt and pepper.

Layer the squash mixture in the bottom of the slow cooker (spreading roughly ½ cup). Top with the lasagna noodles, then more of the squash, the cheese mixture and noodles. Repeat once more, ending with the ricotta mixture. Cover with the mozzarella.

Cook on low for 3-4 hours.

Over-Loaded Baked Potatoes

This versatile baked potato dish can be a standout side or can provide enough sustenance on its own to be a main meal. Not only are baked potatoes great to taste but they are also one of the most potassium-rich foods, helping to keep blood pressure in check, and their skins are high in dietary fiber, helping you get your daily requirement.

Prep Time: 15 minutes
Cook Time: 8 hours
Serves

4 medium russet potatoes
5 cremini mushrooms, trimmed and quartered
2 tablespoons olive oil
1 broccoli, cut into small florets
½ cup low-fat plain yogurt (dairy-free if desired)
Salt and pepper
¼ cup vegetable stock (hot)

Method

Cover the potatoes in foil and place in the slow cooker. Cover and cook on low for 8 hours until the potatoes are cooked thoroughly.

Add the mushrooms to a frying pan and cook with oil for 2 minutes. Add the broccoli and cook until slightly tender.

Cut into the potatoes and scoop out the flesh. In a bowl, combine the flesh, yogurt, seasoning and stock. Once combined, put back into the potato skins and load with the mushroom, broccoli mixture.

Tasty Thai Veg Medley

Spice up your favorite vegetables with this Thai curry recipe. Ideal for both vegetarians and vegans, the combination of squash, peppers, mushrooms and zucchini ensures you're getting a wide variety of flavors and nutrients in one easy-to-prepare meal. As well as having many health benefits, zucchini is well known for helping people lose weight, making this a perfect meal for lunchtimes when combined with the likes of brown rice.

Prep Time: 10 minutes
Cook Time: 3 hours
Serves 4-6

2-3 zucchini, halved lengthwise and cut into 1-inch slices
1 yellow summer squash, cut into 1-inch pieces
1 cup button mushrooms, quartered
1 red pepper, cut into chunks
2 tablespoons vegetable broth
2 cloves garlic, minced
2 tablespoons Thai red curry paste
⅓ cup unsweetened coconut milk
1 tablespoon grated fresh ginger
¼ fresh basil leaves to garnish

Method

Combine all the vegetables in the slow cooker.

Mix the vegetable broth, curry paste and garlic in a bowl. Pour over vegetables and cook on a low heat for 3 hours.

20 minutes before the cooking finishes, stir in the coconut milk and ginger.

Garnish with basil and serve.

White Bean, Carrot and Spinach Salad

Rich in slow-digesting carbohydrates, white beans are the perfect addition to a salad. Especially when combined the nutrients of fresh carrots, spinach and avocado. Top the salad with your favorite nuts — I suggest pistachios — for additional proteins and texture.

Prep Time: 1 hour, 20 minutes
Cook Time: 7-8 hours
Serves 6

1½ cups white beans, rinsed
3 carrots, chopped
1 onion, thinly sliced
2 garlic cloves, minced
½ teaspoon dried oregano
Salt and pepper, to taste
4 cups vegetable stock
1 bag fresh spinach
3 tablespoons lemon juice
1 medium avocado, chopped
Nuts (optional)
Lemon wedges, for serving

Method

Place the beans in a pan with enough water to cover them by 2 inches. Bring to a boil and simmer for 10 minutes. Allow them to stand for 1 hour. Rinse and drain.

Add the beans, carrots, onions, garlic, oregano, salt and pepper to the slow cooker. Cover with the stock and cook on low for 7-8 hours.

Once cooked, drain the mixture and place back in the slow cooker with the spinach and lemon juice. Cover and allow the ingredients to rest for 5 minutes.

If desired, you can set aside some of the cooked juices and drizzle over the salad when served.

Serve the bean mixture with the avocado, nuts and a slice of lemon.

Rich Tempeh Mushroom Stroganoff

Mushrooms are often neglected but provide a wealth of flavor and depth, especially when cooked with a slow cooker. This stroganoff recipe is incredibly simple, has few ingredients and will win you over with its great taste.

With countless studies showing that consuming naturally grown foods like mushrooms decrease the risk of obesity, diabetes and heart disease, there are plenty of reasons why you should give this recipe a go.

Prep Time: 20 minutes
Cook Time: 7-8 hours
Serves 4-6

1 (8 ounce) packet tempeh, cut into 1-centimeter strips
2 cups mushrooms, chopped small
2 cloves garlic, minced
1 to 2 cups water
1 teaspoon Not-Chicken Bouillon
½ teaspoon paprika
⅓ cup vegan sour cream or cashew cream
Salt and pepper, to taste

Method

The recipe is best prepared the night before. Steam the tempeh for 10 minutes (or follow packets instructions) and store in the fridge until morning.

In the morning, add the tempeh, mushrooms, garlic, water, bouillon and paprika to the slow cooker and cook on low for 7-8 hours.

Before serving, add the vegan sour cream and stir. Adjust the seasoning and paprika to your preference, and serve with rice, pasta, cauliflower mash or quinoa.

Creamy & Spicy Coconut Basil Tofu

Fans of tofu will find it hard to resist the allure of this creamy, spicy curry dish. This is a simple recipe that tastes even better the next day, so be sure to make a big batch and just try to resist coming back for seconds!

Prep Time: 15 minutes
Cook Time: 4 hours
Serves 4

2 garlic cloves, minced
1 can coconut milk
1 cup vegetable broth
2 tablespoons tamari
2 tablespoons rice wine vinegar
1 tablespoon fresh ginger, minced
Fresh basil, chopped
1 pack firm tofu, cut into large strips
4 cups baby bok choy, larger pieces cut in half
¾ medium onion, sliced into large pieces
4 mushrooms, sliced
1 tablespoon coconut palm sugar
¼ cup cornstarch
½ teaspoon crushed red pepper flakes
Salt and pepper

Method

Add the garlic, coconut milk, broth, tamari, rice wine vinegar, ginger and basil to the slow cooker and set to low heat.

Place the tofu, vegetables and sugar in the cooker and coat well with the sauce. Cook on high for 3.5 hours. Then add the cornstarch and stir in well.

Cook for another 30 minutes, then season and serve with rice.

Curried Spring Vegetable Stuffed Potato Chaat

This potato chaat is a fantastic dish that will even help you change the minds of non-curry fans. The combination of potatoes, carrots, zucchini and your choice of leafy greens means you have a huge variety of textures and flavors, with all their natural goodness in tow.

There's a subtleness to the spices in the recipe, but they can easily be adapted to suit those who prefer more of a kick with their curries. For the best results, cook the potatoes in the oven before adding to the slow cooker.

Prep Time: 20 minutes
Cook Time: 2-2.5 hours
Serves 4 or 8

Potatoes:
4 medium russet potatoes, cut in half lengthwise
2 teaspoons to 1 tablespoon olive oil
½ teaspoon garam masala or curry powder
¼ teaspoon salt

Curry:
1 tablespoon olive oil
1½ teaspoons garam masala
¼ teaspoon ground cumin
½ teaspoon ground turmeric
¼ teaspoon ground mustard powder
¼ teaspoon ground cinnamon
1 tablespoon grated ginger
1 teaspoon minced garlic
1 cup chopped red bell pepper
1 cup sliced carrots (cut into half moons if very wide)
½ cup water
1 cup diced zucchini
2 cups chopped rainbow chard (or other green, like kale or spinach)
Salt to taste

Method

For the potatoes:
Preheat your oven to 425° and line a baking tray with parchment paper. Rub the potatoes with olive oil and place on baking tray cut side down. Sprinkle with the garam masala and salt. Cook for 30 to 45 minutes.

Allow potatoes to cool, then scoop out their middles, leaving enough potato behind in the skin to make a firm bowl.

For the curry:
Add the oil, garam masala, cumin, turmeric, mustard and cinnamon to the slow cooker on high. Allow to heat and then add the ginger, garlic and pepper and cook further.

Add the carrots and water, and then cook for 30 minutes with the lid on. Then add the potato, zucchini and greens, and continue to cook. If it looks as though the mixture is sticking, then add some water. Allow to cook for another 1 hour to 1.5 hours.

Cooking time depends on your slow cooker, but as the potato is already cooked, judge it on how much of a bite you like your veg to have.

Once done, scoop the contents into the potato skins and serve with a dollop of yogurt and fresh cut herbs.

Tempeh Braised with Figs and Port Wine

Tempeh is an Indonesian cultured soy food that provides probiotics that promote healthy digestion and immune systems. It also lends itself surprisingly well to slow cooker recipes, making it an ideal substitution for any non-vegan or non-vegetarian recipes.

Here we're being a little indulgent and enjoying it with juicy figs and port wine.

Prep Time: 10 minutes
Cook Time: 6-8 hours
Serves 4

2 tablespoons olive oil
1 small onion, minced
2 cloves garlic, minced
1 (8 ounce) package tempeh, cubed
8 fresh figs, each cut into 6 wedges
1 cup port wine
1/2 cup water
1 tablespoon balsamic vinegar
1 tablespoon vegan bouillon
1 sprig fresh rosemary
1 sprig fresh thyme
Salt and pepper, to taste

Method

The night before, heat the oil in a frying pan on medium heat, sauté the onion until it becomes translucent and add the garlic for a further minute. Add them to the tempeh and figs in an airtight container and put in the fridge overnight.

In the morning add all the ingredients into the slow cooker and cook for 6 to 8 hours on low.

Hearty Irish Stew

Irish stew is a comforting and hearty meal that you can compare to having a warm hug on a cold winter's day. This recipe is best when it utilizes seasonal root vegetables and tastes amazing when served with cauliflower mash.

Like any stew there is no right or wrong recipe, so feel free to customize it toward your preferences and try new things. It's an incredibly flexible recipe, whether you want to be fancy and sauté or just throw all the ingredients into your cooker and come back to it once it's cooked.

Prep Time: 10 minutes
Cook Time: 6-8 hours
Serves 6

1 onion (white or red), diced
2 cloves garlic, finely chopped
3 large potatoes, peeled and cut into chunks
2 large carrots, peeled and cut into chunks
2 large parsnips, peeled and cut into chunks
1 celery stem, cut into chunks
4 cups vegetable broth at room temperature
¾ cup apple juice or cider
¼ cup apple cider vinegar
3 tablespoons pearl barley
½ teaspoon dried sage or 3 fresh sage leaves finely chopped
1 bay leaf
½ cup frozen peas, thawed
Salt and pepper to taste

Method

Sauté the onion and garlic in a pan until soft and place in cooker (optional).

Add all the ingredients except peas to the slow cooker. Cover and cook on low for 6 to 8 hours. Add the peas for the final hour.

Serve in a bowl with crusty bread or mash.

Jambalaya

Jambalaya, which is French for "jumbled," is a dish that lends itself perfectly to slow cooking. Typically a dish made of strong flavors and great textures, this recipe is a combination of rice, colorful vegetables and a spicy kick.

Okra is the star of the show in this recipe, bringing you the usual high amount of dietary fiber you expect from vegetables, as well as being rich in vitamins A, C and antioxidants. All of which will not only make you look healthy but feel healthy too, as okra has been linked to cough and cold prevention.

Prep Time: 10 minutes
Cook Time: 4-6 hours
Serves 4

1 cup okra, cubed
1 green bell pepper
½ onion
3 celery ribs (about 1½ cups)
1 (16 ounce) can diced tomatoes & green chilis
1½ cups vegetable broth
2 cloves garlic, minced
½ teaspoon paprika
¼ teaspoon salt
¼ teaspoon ground black pepper
¼ teaspoon cayenne pepper
3 cups cooked cilantro rice
6 ounces soy chorizo (optional)

Method

Add all the vegetables to the slow cooker and pour in the tomatoes and vegetable broth.

Add the garlic and seasoning and give the jambalaya a good stir.

Cook on low for 4-6 hours. Mix in the cooked rice before serving.

Rice, Feta and Kalamata Olives

A perfect dish for summer, Greek rice fits right in at BBQs, as a salad feature or as a vegetarian main dish. The combination of lemon, black pepper and garlic creates a vibrant and fresh taste.

Prep Time: 15 minutes
Cook Time: 2 hours
Serves 4-6

1¾ cups rice
1 tablespoon olive oil
1 onion, chopped small
1 teaspoon minced garlic
1 teaspoon dried oregano
3 cups vegetable stock
1 red bell pepper, seeds removed and finely chopped
¾ cup sliced Kalamata olives
¾ cup crumbled feta cheese
1 tablespoon fresh-squeezed lemon juice
¼ cup finely chopped fresh parsley

Method

Sauté the rice with the oil in a frying pan until browned. Add the rice to the slow cooker.

Add the onion, garlic and oregano to the same frying pan, and brown. Add the stock and ensure you scrape all the tasty brown bits off the pan. Add this stock mixture to the slow cooker. Cook for 1½ hours on high.

Once the rice has softened (around the 1½ hour mark) add the peppers and cook for a further 15 minutes. Then add the olives and feta and cook for a further 15 minutes.

Serve with a squeeze of lemon and fresh parsley.

Healthy and Filling Lentil-Quinoa Tacos

If you're a fan of Mexican food, then this lentil-quinoa taco filling is guaranteed to impress. The combination of smoked paprika and chili powder gives the lentils a wonderful BBQ feel and of course you're getting the benefit of the lentil's high folate, fiber and protein without the hassle of cooking them on the stove.

Prep Time: 5 minutes
Cook Time: 7-9 hours
Serves 3-6

¼ cup brown lentils
¼ cup beluga lentils or brown lentils
¼ cup quinoa, rinsed
2 cloves garlic, minced
2 cups water
½ teaspoon chili powder
½ teaspoon smoked paprika
6 soft or hard corn taco shells
Salt and pepper, to taste

Method

Add all the ingredients except the tacos and salt and pepper to the cooker. Cook on low for 7-9 hours.

Season to taste and serve in the taco shells with lettuce, avocado, tomatoes and lime.

Best Meat-Free Lentil Bolognese

If you're after a meat-free alternative for your Bolognese, then lentils are the ideal alternative. Meaty in their consistency, lentils are a good source of iron, something that all vegetarians should be looking to include in their diets.

The combination of lentils and mushrooms provides the texture and flavor that make this Bolognese an incredibly satisfying meal — and even tastier the next day.

Prep Time: 15 minutes
Cook Time: 4 hours
Serves 4

3 cloves garlic, minced
1 cup brown lentils
1 stalk celery, chopped
2 carrots, chopped
4 white mushrooms, chopped
½ cup red wine
1 shallot, minced
¼ cup organic tomato paste
1 can diced organic tomatoes
2 tablespoons extra virgin olive oil
2 cups vegetable broth
1 bay leaf
¼ teaspoon Italian seasonings
⅛ teaspoon ground nutmeg
Salt and pepper to taste

Method

In a frying pan, sauté the shallot and garlic. Add the celery, carrots and mushrooms until the mushrooms begin to brown. Add the wine to the pan and simmer. Transfer the pan's contents to the slow cooker.

Add the remaining ingredients to the slow cooker and cook on high for 4 hours, or until the lentils are soft.

Slow-Cooked Tofu in Pineapple Barbecue Sauce

Naturally gluten-free and low in calories, tofu is a perfect alternative to meat. This barbecue sauce recipe does away with all those hidden sugar and sodium bombs you find in packaged sauces. The pineapple adds a zing and freshness to the dish that screams summer.

Prep Time: 15 minutes
Cook Time: 8 hours
Serves 4-6

2 (14 ounce) packets extra-firm tofu
1 large onion, chopped
8 large cloves garlic, minced
1½ cups crushed pineapple in own juice
2 fresh hot chili peppers, chopped
3 tablespoons ginger, minced
5 tablespoons tomato paste
⅓ cup water
2 tablespoons tamari or lite soy sauce
1 tablespoon lime juice
1 tablespoon cider vinegar
Salt (optional) and pepper

Method

A day or more before you plan to cook this dish, freeze the tofu. This helps keep the tofu firmer and makes it more resilient when cooked. Remove from the freezer and defrost in the fridge.

When defrosted, cut each block into quarters. Squeeze any excess liquid out of the tofu and cut into ½ inch cubes.

Add the onion and garlic to a frying pan or the sauté option of your slow cooker. Add this mixture and all the remaining ingredients except the tofu into a blender and blend until a consistent texture.

Add the tofu to the slow cooker and pour over the sauce. Ensure all sides of the tofu is covered. Cook on low for 8 hours. Check occasionally.

Season to taste and serve with a fresh salad.

A Slow-Cooked Puttanesca Pizza

If you've tried the pizza bread recipe, then perhaps you're beginning to consider that slow cooker pizza is an actual possibility. This vegan puttanesca pizza is a relatively hassle-free and delicious recipe that can be customized with all your favorite toppings.

Prep Time: 1 hour, 30 minutes
Cook Time: 1 hour, 45 minutes
Serves 2

Dough:
1½ cups unbleached all-purpose flour
1½ teaspoon instant yeast
½ teaspoon salt
½ teaspoon Italian seasoning
1 tablespoon olive oil
½ cup warm water

Sauce:
½ cup crushed tomatoes
¼ cup pitted green olives, sliced
¼ teaspoon dried basil
¼ teaspoon dried oregano
¼ teaspoon garlic powder
¼ teaspoon sugar
¼ teaspoon hot red pepper flakes
1 tablespoon chopped fresh flat-leaf parsley
½ cup shredded vegan mozzarella cheese (optional)
Salt and freshly ground black pepper

Method

For the dough:
Oil the inside of a large bowl. Mix the flour, yeast, salt and seasoning in a food processor. Add the oil as it mixes and the water gradually to make a slightly sticky dough.

Knead the dough with flour for 2 minutes until smooth. Add the dough to the oiled bowl and turn to coat. Cover and set the bowl aside for 1 hour.

For the sauce:
While the dough rises, combine the tomatoes, olives, herbs and seasoning into a bowl.

Flatten the dough on a floured surface and shape so it just fits inside the slow cooker. Oil the inside of the slow cooker and add the dough. Spread the sauce over the dough. Place a clean kitchen towel under the cooker's lid to prevent condensation. Cook on high for 1 hour, 15 minutes. Add the cheese and cook for a further 30 minutes.

The Best Alternative Butternut Squash Macaroni

A perfect comfort food, this butternut squash macaroni gives a silky and cleaner alternative to the usual mac and cheese. Squash is a favorite for people looking to control cholesterol and reduce weight, plus it's low calorie and rich in nutrients that benefit everything from your bones to your hair.

Prep Time: 15-20 minutes
Cook Time: 8-9 hours
Serves 5

For the morning:
1½ cups cubed butternut squash
½ cup chopped tomatoes
1½ cups water
2 cloves garlic, minced
Fresh thyme or 1½ teaspoons dried thyme
Fresh rosemary or ½ teaspoon dried rosemary

For the evening:
¼ cup nutritional yeast flakes
½ to 1 cup almond milk, divided
1½ cups uncooked whole-wheat macaroni
Salt and pepper, to taste

Method

For the morning:
Add the morning ingredients to the slow cooker. Cook on low for 7-8 hours.

45 minutes before serving:
Puree the contents of the slow cooker with the yeast flakes and half the milk. Add the mixture back to the slow cooker with the pasta. Cover and cook for 20 minutes.

Check the mixture, adding more milk if required. Cook for another 20 or so minutes until the pasta is al dente.

Season to taste and serve.

Comforting Root Veggie Barley Risotto

Risottos are usually associated with lots of effort and inconsistent results, but slow cookers make them an absolute pleasure. Not only because you simply have to throw all the ingredients in but the end result will also wow friends and family. Barley is an underused grain that is vitamin and mineral-rich, making it well worth introducing into your diet. The addition of root vegetables not only makes the risotto nourishing but also an ultimate comfort food.

Prep Time: 10 minutes
Cook Time: 7-8 hours
Serves 3-4

½ cup barley
2 carrots, diced
½ cup turnip, diced
½ cup diced sweet potatoes
2 cloves garlic, minced
2 cups water
½ teaspoon dried oregano
½ teaspoon dried sage
1 cup minced greens (collards, kale, etc.)
Salt and pepper, to taste
½ teaspoon lemon zest

Method

Add all the ingredients except the greens, salt and pepper, and lemon zest to the slow cooker and cook on low for 7 to 8 hours.

Just before serving, add the greens and lemon zest. Season to taste and serve.

Stew Recipes

West African Sweet Potato and Peanut Stew

This is a creamy and smooth stew that is not only super easy but also perfect for those peanut butter lovers out there. It is a satisfying recipe that can be easily customized with whatever you have lying around your cupboards. Peanut butter brings a depth to this dish and is also a heart-friendly and protein-rich food.

Prep Time: 10 minutes
Cook Time: 6 hours
Serves 4-6

1 large sweet potato, peeled and cubed
1 small white onion, peeled and diced ½ cup peanut butter (smooth or crunchy)
2 cloves garlic, minced
1 can diced tomatoes with juice
4 cups water
1 teaspoon grated fresh ginger
¼-½ teaspoon ground chipotle pepper
1 teaspoon smoked paprika
½ teaspoon salt
4 cups fresh baby spinach

Method

Combine all ingredients except the spinach in the slow cooker. Cook on low for 6 hours. Once the sweet potatoes become tender towards the end of cooking, stir in the spinach, letting it cook for 10 minutes. Season and serve.

Veg & Aduki Bean Stew

Aduki beans are an excellent addition to a stew. Not only are they a good quality source of protein but they also provide a sweet and nutty texture, which is guaranteed to sate your appetite after a long day of work.

Prep Time: 10 minutes
Cook Time: 4-6 hours
Serves 6

250 grams dried aduki beans, soaked overnight in cold water
1 large onion
6 garlic cloves, peeled and chopped
1 leek, chopped
1 sweet potato, chopped
2 pints water
2 teaspoons freshly ground black pepper
8 brussels sprouts, halved
A bunch of kale, spinach or other greens, chopped

Method

It is important to soak the aduki beans overnight, following the packaging's instructions.

Add all the ingredients except the brussels sprouts and greens to the slow cooker, and cook for 4-6 hours on high.

Around 30 minutes before cooking finishes, add the sprouts and greens (note spinach will require much less time), and season well before serving.

Easy Saag Aloo

Saag Aloo is an Indian dish that provides a good deal of nutritious spinach and nourishment from its other main ingredient, potatoes. The combination of these two ingredients and spices makes for a warming and comforting dish that is ideal for any vegetarian's plate.

Prep Time: 10 minutes
Cook Time: 3 hours
Serves 4-6

650 grams potatoes, peeled and cut into 1-inch pieces½ onion, thinly sliced
½ vegetable stock cube, crumbled
50ml water
1 tablespoon oil
½ teaspoon cumin
½ teaspoon ground coriander
½ teaspoon garam masala
½ teaspoon hot chilli powder
Black pepper
250 grams fresh spinach, roughly chopped

Method

Add all the ingredients except the spinach to the slow cooker, and cook on high for 3 hours. Around the last hour mark, add a good few handfuls of spinach to the cooker, gently combining.

When the potato is soft, it is ready to serve.

Versatile Vegetable Stew

This is a delicious, nutrient-rich stew, packed full of vegetables. It not only makes for perfect comfort food but you'll also be getting a good deal of your recommended daily nutritional requirements. Throw in whatever vegetables you or your family love to eat and watch them go back for seconds.

Prep Time: 10 minutes
Cook Time: 8 hours
Serves 6

1 medium onion, sliced
1 carrot, sliced
1 celery stalk, sliced
1 medium sweet potato, cubed
1 russet potato, cubed
4 cups kale, chopped
4 cloves garlic, minced
1 teaspoon seasoning
1 can diced tomatoes
2 cups pumpkin
4 cups vegetable broth
Salt and pepper, to taste

Method

Add everything to the slow cooker and cook on low for 8 hours. Use less broth if you prefer a thicker stew.

New Mexican Pozole

Pozole is a traditional hominy Mexican soup or stew. Savory and hearty, it has a nice kick to it thanks to the jalapenos, making it perfect for those times when you're feeling a little under the weather. Hominy consists of dried maize kernels and is a rich source of vitamins, antioxidants and minerals, making a great addition to your diet.

Prep Time: 15 minutes
Cook Time: 4.5 hours
Serves 4-6

2 poblano peppers, seeded if you don't want too much heat
2 jalapenos, seeded
1 pound tomatillos
1 cup cilantro
4 cloves garlic, minced
1 tablespoon dried oregano
Salt and pepper to taste
8 cups vegetable broth, divided
60 ounces canned hominy, drained
3 zucchini, chopped

Method

Add the poblano peppers, jalapenos, tomatillos, cilantro, garlic, oregano, salt and pepper, and 1 cup vegetable broth to a blender and mix until smooth.

Season well and then put in the slow cooker. Cook on low for 4 hours. Add the zucchini for 30 further minutes.

Black Beans and Tomatoes

Black beans are an exceptional source of nutrients and also have a wide variety of health benefits associated with them. From lowering blood sugar levels to keeping you satisfied for longer, beans should never be overlooked in a vegetarian or vegan diet. This dish is a tasty and inexpensive meal, making it ideal if you want a hearty meal on a budget.

Prep Time: 5-10 minutes
Cook Time: 4-5 hours
Serves 8

2 cups dry black beans
1 can diced tomatoes
1 medium jalapeno, diced
4 cloves garlic, minced
½ tablespoon cumin
5 cups water
Salt to taste

Method

Rinse the beans, then add to the slow cooker with the other ingredients except the salt.

Cover and cook for 4 hours. Check the beans to see if they are tender, if not continue cooking and check regularly. Season with salt and serve.

Sweet & Spicy Baked Beans

An ideal recipe to make in your cooker, slow-cooked baked beans provide a firm but creamy texture that is perfectly complemented by a sweet-and-spicy sauce. Navy beans are an excellent source of fiber, containing 19 grams per serving, and can also help in energy production and keeping your brain staying sharp. Try serving these with crusty bread or loaded on jacket potatoes.

Prep Time: 5-10 minutes
Cook Time: 6 hours
Serves 6-8

1 pound dried navy beans
1 medium onion, finely chopped
2 garlic cloves, minced
⅓ cup cider vinegar
½ cup barbecue sauce or ketchup
½ cup packed light-brown sugar
2 tablespoons Dijon mustard
2½ cups water
¼ teaspoon hot sauce, if desired
Salt and pepper

Method

Cover the beans in water and allow to soak overnight or for at least 8 hours. Drain the beans and put them in the cooker.

Mix all the other ingredients in a bowl and add to the slow cooker. Stir until thoroughly combined.

Cover and cook on low for 6 hours or until the beans are tender.

Season as required, and then serve.

Bean, Artichoke and Chard Ragout

This ragout provides the mellow flavors of slow-cooked beans and artichokes, with the crunch of raw fennel and peppers nestled on top. The combination of veggies in this dish makes for a powerhouse of nutrients and goodness. You'll be getting a good amount of dietary fiber, iron and vitamins, which will definitely leave you feeling satisfied. It can even be prepared a day before and left in the fridge until you're ready to cook it.

Prep Time: 20 minutes
Cook Time: 4 hours
Serves 6

Ragout:
3 cups thinly sliced leek
1 cup carrot, sliced
3 garlic cloves, minced
3 cups cooked cannellini beans
2 cups cubed red potato
1 cup chopped red bell pepper
1 teaspoon dried basil
¼ teaspoon dried oregano
Salt and black pepper
1 (14.5 ounce) can diced tomatoes with basil, garlic and oregano, drained
1¾ cups organic vegetable broth
1 (9 ounce) package frozen artichoke hearts, thawed
¾ cup water
1 tablespoon olive oil
2 cups chopped Swiss chard

Relish:
1 cup boiling water
6 sun-dried tomatoes, without oil
3 cups shredded fennel bulb
1 cup diced yellow bell pepper
¼ cup chopped fresh parsley
1 tablespoon fresh lemon juice
2 teaspoons olive oil
½ teaspoon sugar
Salt and black pepper

Method

Add the leek, carrot and garlic to a frying pan and heat for 5 minutes. Transfer contents to the slow cooker.

Add all the ingredients except the chard for the ragout to the cooker. Cover and cook on high for 8 hours, or until tender. Add the chard at the end, and stop cooking once wilted.

For the relish, combine the water and tomatoes; allow them to sit for 15 minutes. Drain, then chop and combine with the remaining ingredients. Serve on top of the ragout.

Creamy and Sweet Vegetable Korma

This vegetable korma is an indulgent and flavorful curry that all the family will love. Packed with vegetables, this is nutritional comfort food at its best. There's all the goodness without the need for added oils and fat.

Prep Time: 5-10 minutes
Cook Time: 8 hours
Serves 4-6

1 cauliflower, cut into florets
½ cup frozen peas
2 carrots, chopped
½ onion, chopped
2 cloves garlic, minced
¾ can coconut milk
2 tablespoons curry powder
1 tablespoon red pepper flakes
1 teaspoon garam masala
2 tablespoons coconut flour (to thicken)
Salt and pepper

Method

Add the cauliflower, peas, carrots, onion and garlic to the slow cooker (add or sub in any other vegetables you'd like) and mix together.

In a large bowl, combine the coconut milk and other seasonings, mixing well. Pour over the vegetables and add the coconut flour.

Cook on low for 8 hours and serve when the curry has thickened.

"Game Day" Vegan Slow Cooker Sloppy Joes

A meatless sloppy Joe recipe that is guaranteed to convert even the biggest meat-lover, lentils or kidney beans are the main ingredient, providing a nice texture, taste and plenty of nutrition. From being an energy booster to rich in protein and fiber, kidney beans are a filling legume that is a perfect staple for any vegetarian.

Prep Time: 5 minutes
Cook Time: 5-6 hours
Serves 8

2 cans no-salt red kidney beans, drained
2 large onions, chopped
2 large red bell peppers, chopped
1 can fire-roasted or regular tomato sauce
8 cloves of garlic, minced
¼ cup organic ketchup
1 tablespoon Dijon mustard
1 teaspoon chipotle or chili powder
½ teaspoon cumin
½ teaspoon smoked paprika
8 buns or rolls, to serve

Method

Add the ingredients to the slow cooker. Cook on low for 5-6 hours. Mash a side of the stew to help thicken the sauce. Judge how much you mash by how thick you like your sloppy Joes.

Serve in the buns.

Soup Recipes

Lazy Leek & Potato soup

Leek and potato soup is a satisfying and nutritious meal that won't have you reaching for the cookie tin any time soon. Leeks are a versatile vegetable that are easy to prepare and packed full of vitamins A and K. Whether you choose to go rustic or blend the soup, you can end up with a fantastic texture and combination of flavors that you're guaranteed to enjoy.

Prep Time: 10 minutes
Cook Time: 4 hours
Serves 5-6

2 large leeks, thinly sliced
4 large potatoes, peeled and cubed
2 carrots, chopped
2 celery stalks, chopped
2 cloves garlic, minced
4 to 6 cups vegetable broth
Salt and pepper to taste
Fresh parsley to garnish
Heavy or coconut cream (optional)

Method

The size you cut the vegetables depends entirely on your taste and whether you'd rather have a chunky soup or blended. If you aren't going to blend the soup, then quarter the potatoes rather than cutting them into cubes.

After preparing all the vegetables, place them into the slow cooker. Add the garlic and vegetable broth, ensuring that there is enough to cover all the veggies.

Place the lid on the cooker and cook for 4 hours on a high heat.

Blend the mixture if you'd like and add a spoonful of cream for extra thickness if you'd like. Garnish with chopped parsley and season with salt and pepper to taste.

Super Kale, Lentil & Potato Soup

Kale is among the most nutrient-dense foods in the planet, so you should be looking to sneak it into your family's meals wherever possible. Combine with lentils and you have a soup that provides you with high-quality protein and fiber.

My version of kale, lentil and potato soup is not only quick to prepare but it offers a great deal of flavor and goodness.

Prep Time: 10 minutes
Cook Time: 6-7 hours
Serves 6

1 bunch of kale, stems removed and cut into bite size pieces
1 celery stick, sliced
1 carrot, sliced
1 onion, chopped
3 potatoes, cubed into inch pieces
1 cup dried lentils, rinsed
2 garlic cloves, minced
6 cups vegetable broth
1 tablespoon thyme
1 tablespoon sage
Salt and pepper to taste

Method

Add the vegetables, lentils and garlic to the slow cooker. Cover the mixture with the broth and add in the seasoning, stir to combine, and then cook on low heat for 6-7 hours.

For an extra oomph, just before the soup has finished cooking, you can steam any remaining kale until tender and add it to the soup.

Wintery Parsnip and Butternut Squash Soup

Velvety in consistency, rich in color and deep in flavor, this parsnip and butternut squash soup is ideal for those gloomier days where you long for comfort food. The addition of parsnips helps bring an edge and kick to an otherwise sweet soup, as well as a healthy quantity of fiber and folate, which is great for keeping the nervous system healthy.

Once you've added the parsnip you'll wonder why it hasn't been a mainstay in all your soups. Keep in mind the core of can be quite tough but will become tender with the slow cooker. You may want to play around with using more or less of the core, depending on your preference.

Prep Time: 10 minutes
Cook Time: 6 hours
Serves 3-4

1 small butternut squash, cubed
2 parsnips, peeled and chopped
1 onion chopped
2 cups vegetable broth
½ teaspoon cilantro
½ teaspoon cumin powder
Salt and pepper to taste
½ tablespoon chopped ginger (optional)

Method

Add all of the ingredients into the slow cooker, ensuring there is enough broth to cover the vegetables, and cook on low heat for 6 hours. If you're looking for even more of a kick from your soup, then add some chopped ginger.

Check the vegetables are cooked thoroughly before blending the contents and serving with some crusty bread.

Roast Garlic Revamped Tomato Soup

One of the most popular and feel-good soups, this tomato soup gets a wake-up call with a good amount of roast garlic. Garlic is renowned for its healing qualities, making it a nice partner for tomato soup and when you're feeling a little run down.

The soup has a wonderfully intense flavor, with the garlic and tomatoes perfectly complementing each other.

Prep Time: 10 minutes
Cook Time: 3-4 hours
Serves 4-6

1 head garlic
30 ounces ripe tomatoes
1 can diced tomato
1 small/medium white onion, diced
½ cup vegetable broth 1 teaspoon sugar
Salt and pepper
2 tablespoons heavy cream or coconut cream (optional)
Fresh basil to serve

Method

Cut the head off of the garlic and roast in the oven for 20-25 minutes until the cloves begin to caramelize. Allow to cool and remove the cloves from their cases.

Bring a large pot of water to the boil and add the tomatoes. Boil for 3 minutes, drain and run cold water over them until they are cool enough to remove the skin and cores.

Add all the ingredients to the slow cooker, except the cream and basil. Cook on high for 3-4 hours.

When cooking is finished, use an immersion blender to smooth the soup. Stir in the cream if you'd like a creamier texture, season and garnish with basil to serve.

Spiced Curried Vegetable and Chickpea Soup

A favorite of mine, this creamy curried soup is full of tender vegetables and chickpeas. If you're after a warming and tasty soup, then this is the one for you.

It is an ideal recipe for clearing out the fridge and can be filled with whichever vegetables you have lying around.

All the vegetables makes for a nutrient-rich soup and the addition of fresh ginger packs some strong medicinal qualities. This makes for a fairly chunky soup but can be blended if preferred.

Prep Time: 15-20 minutes
Cook Time: 4 hours
Serves 8-10

1 teaspoon olive oil
1 large onion, diced
2 medium red or yellow potatoes, diced
3 garlic cloves, minced
1-inch piece ginger, peeled and grated
1 tablespoon curry powder
1 tablespoon brown sugar
2 cups vegetable broth
1 medium head of cauliflower, cut into bite-size florets
2 cans chickpeas, drained and rinsed
1 can chopped tomatoes
1 green bell pepper, diced
Salt and pepper
1 (10 ounce) bag baby spinach
1 cup coconut milk

Method

Add the oil to a frying pan and sauté the onion until it becomes slightly translucent. Add the potatoes and sauté for a further 5 minutes. Stir in the garlic, ginger, curry powder and brown sugar until the vegetables are coated. Pour in enough of the vegetable broth to allow you to loosen up all the crispy bits from the pan.

Transfer the pan's contents to the slow cooker.

Add the rest of the ingredients except the spinach and coconut milk, and stir to combine. The vegetables should just be covered; you can always add more broth if necessary.

Cook on high for 4 hours.

Just before the cooking has finished, stir in the spinach and coconut milk.

Covering for a few minutes so the spinach wilts.

Perfectly Morish Cauliflower & Sweet Potato Bisque

This soup has a great texture and depth to it. If you're partial to a slight sweetness in your soups, then the combination of cauliflower and sweet potato provides a rich and full flavor that will definitely satisfy.

Although it contains both cauliflower and sweet potato, the soup is actually quite light, making it ideal for lunch or thickened with cream for a heartier dinnertime meal. The potato provides ideal slow-release energy, and cauliflower contains plenty of vitamin and minerals, as well as essential dietary fiber, keeping you healthy and happy.

Prep Time: 10 minutes
Cook Time: 3-4 hours
Serves 4

1 cauliflower, cut into florets
2 sweet potato, peeled and cubed
1 onion, diced
2 cloves garlic, minced
1½ cups vegetable broth
½ teaspoon dried thyme
½ teaspoon chili flakes
½ cup almond milk
1 tablespoon coconut cream (optional)
Salt and pepper

Method

Add the cauliflower, sweet potato, onion, garlic, broth, thyme and flakes into the slow cooker and heat on high for 3-4 hours.

At the end of cooking, add the milk and coconut cream if desired. Use an immersion blender or food processer until the soup is smooth. Season to taste and serve immediately with crusty bread and a green-onion garnish.

Corn & Red Pepper Chowder

Corn chowder is a comforting food that hits all the right spots on those cold and rainy days. The addition of red pepper makes for a hearty, creamy and flavorful chowder that the whole family will love. I've intentionally made this recipe lighter than others, steering clear of the unnecessary cheese and dairy-heavy options you'll find with other recipes.

Allow it to simmer in the slow cooker all day, and you'll have a chowder that keeps getting better with time.

Prep Time: 10 minutes
Cook Time: 8.5 hours
Serves 4-6

1 medium yellow onion, diced
2 tablespoons olive oil
1 medium red bell pepper, seeded and diced
3 medium Yukon Gold potatoes, diced
4 cups frozen sweet corn kernels, divided (or fresh corn)
4 cups vegetable broth
1 teaspoon ground cumin
½ teaspoon smoked paprika
⅛ teaspoon cayenne pepper
1 teaspoon kosher salt
1 cup almond milk
Salt and pepper to taste

Method

Add the onion and oil to a frying pan and sauté. Add this to the slow cooker with the pepper, potatoes, 3 cups of corn, broth and seasoning.

Cook on low for 8 hours, until the potatoes are tender.

Once cooked, use a blender to puree the soup, stir in the almond milk and remaining corn. Cook for a further 30 minutes, and serve.

Easy Peasy Split-Pea Soup

This quick and simple soup is a healthy and hearty meal that requires very little effort. Perfect for those of us who love a traditional pea soup, this dish will keep you full and content for a good chunk of the day thanks to one cup containing 65% of your required dietary fiber for the day.

Serve with some crispy bread to keep you going even longer.

Prep Time: 5 minutes
Cook Time: 4-5 hours high/8 hours low
Serves 6-8

3 large carrots, diced
2 cups yellow split peas
1 large white onion, sliced
3 cloves of garlic, crushed
1 bay leaf
½ teaspoon thyme
Salt and pepper, to taste
7 cups hot water

Method

Add all the ingredients to the slow cooker and combine.

Cover and cook for 8 hours on low or 4-5 hours on high, until the peas are soft.

Season to taste and serve.

Winter Vegetable Soup

Seasonal vegetables are a great way to keep you and the family fit and healthy throughout the different times of the year. This winter soup is full of all the vegetables that will help keep you energized and ensure your immune system is running at its best, keeping those pesky colds and flu at bay.

Prep Time: 10 minutes
Cook Time: 8 hours, 20 minutes
Serves 8

4 medium red potatoes, cut into ½-inch cubes
4 medium stalks celery, cubed
3 medium carrots, cubed
2 medium parsnips, peeled and cut into chunks
2 medium leeks, cut into ½-inch pieces
2 cans diced tomatoes with Italian herbs, with juice
1 cup (14 ounces) vegetable broth
½ teaspoon dried thyme leaves
½ teaspoon dried rosemary leaves
½ teaspoon salt
3 tablespoons cornstarch
3 tablespoons water

Method

Add all the ingredients except the cornstarch and water into the slow cooker.

Cook on low for 8 hours. Mix the water and cornstarch in a bowl, and gradually stir into the soup until blended. Cook for a further 20 minutes on high, stir occasionally to thicken.

Vibrant and Healthy Carrot and Caramelized Onion Soup

A gluten and dairy-free soup, my carrot and caramelized onion soup is bristling with flavor and sweetness. Perfect for a rainy day or if you're having sugar cravings. Carrots are also a great way to give your body a vitamin A boost and have a host of other powerful health benefits.

Prep Time: 30 minutes
Cook Time: 8 hours
Serves 8

2½ pounds carrots peeled and sliced into coins
2 large onions, sliced
3 tablespoons olive oil
1 large Yukon gold potato, peeled and cubed
½ cup celery sliced
16 ounces vegetable stock
Salt and pepper to taste
Cilantro to garnish

Method

Caramelize the onions in a frying pan over low heat until golden brown (30 minutes).

Add all the ingredients to the slow cooker and cook on low for 8 hours or until the vegetables are tender. Blend with an immersion blender until it reaches your preferred texture, and serve with a cilantro garnish.

Hearty Bean Soup

This recipe uses large white northern beans that offer a mild but distinct flavor and plenty of distinct health benefits. A serving of these beans will give you 15 grams of protein, as well as plenty of fiber and iron. Throw in the rest of the ingredients and you have a healthy and filling soup that is ideal for anytime of the week.

Prep Time: 5 minutes
Cook Time: 5 hours
Serves

1 pound dry Great Northern Beans (if using cooked beans, add halfway through cooking)
1 small onion, finely chopped
3 carrots, peeled and finely chopped
2 celery stems, finely chopped
1 tablespoon fennel seeds
2 teaspoons dried oregano leaves
2 teaspoons garlic powder
¼ teaspoon red pepper flakes (optional)
Salt and pepper to taste

Method

Combine the beans, onion, carrots, celery, fennel, oregano, garlic and pepper flakes and cold water to the slow cooker.

Cook on high for 5 hours, until the beans are tender. Add enough water to achieve your desired thickness, add salt and pepper to taste, and serve.

Chunky and Rich Minestrone Soup

Minestrone is a thick soup, originating from Italy and usually includes either pasta or rice. Don't let the long list of ingredients intimidate you though! Most are a variety of dried or fresh herbs for seasoning. Of course when it comes to vegetables, the more the merrier.

The hearty combination of vegetables and pasta makes this the perfect lunchtime soup that will help fuel you for the rest of the day. Choose your preferred pasta — you can even add filled tortellini if you like — and you have created a satisfying and hearty meal.

Prep Time: 15 minutes
Cook Time: 8-9 hours
Serves 6-8

2 cans diced tomatoes
1 cup diced celery
1 cup diced carrots
1 cup diced yellow onion
4 cups vegetable stock
2 tablespoons chopped fresh parsley (or dried)
2 teaspoons dried basil
1 teaspoon dried oregano
½ teaspoon dried thyme
¾ teaspoon dried rosemary, crushed
2 bay leaves
½ teaspoon sugar
1⅓ cups diced zucchini
1⅓ cups shell pasta
4 cloves garlic, minced
1 can dark red kidney beans, drained and rinsed
1 can white navy beans or cannellini beans, drained and rinsed
1 can Italian green beans, drained
2 cups water
Salt and freshly ground black pepper, to taste
Finely shredded Romano cheese, for serving (optional)

Method

Add the vegetables except the zucchini and green beans, stock, parsley, basil, oregano, thyme, rosemary, bay leaves and sugar to your slow cooker (use smaller quantities for smaller cookers). Cook on low for 6-8 hours.

Add the zucchini, pasta, garlic, and kidney and navy beans, cook on high for an additional 30-40 minutes, until the beans and pasta are tender. Add the green beans for the last 10 minutes. Thin with additional broth Romano cheese if preferred, and serve.

Thai-Inspired Butternut Squash and Peanut Soup

Butternut squash is a regular in soup recipes and for good reason! The vegetable not only packs a lot of nutritional benefit, but it also provides a rich and slightly nutty flavor that complements a lot of other flavors.

This Thai-inspired soup is just want you'll need when it's time to add some life to your soup. The combination of ginger, pepper and curry paste adds warmth that is perfect for colder days.

Prep Time: 20 minutes
Cook Time: 3 hours
Serves 4-6

2 pounds peeled and cubed butternut squash
1 cup vegetable stock
1 onion, finely chopped
2 teaspoons olive oil
2 teaspoons minced garlic
1 teaspoon minced ginger root
1 red bell pepper, seeds removed and finely chopped
1 (14 ounce) can coconut milk
2 tablespoons Thai red curry paste
½ cup peanut butter
2 teaspoons vegan fish sauce
1 tablespoon brown sugar
⅓ cup cilantro, finely chopped
2 tablespoons fresh-squeezed lime juice
Salt and pepper to taste

Method

You can prepare the butternut squash using my whole butternut squash recipe, or if using pre-cubed pieces, add the squash to the slow cooker with the stock, seasoning generously and cooking on high for 2 hours.

Use a blender to puree the squash.

In a large frying pan, sauté the onion in oil until browned. Add the garlic, ginger, pepper and sauté further. Add the coconut milk, curry paste and peanut butter until the mixture has melted. Add the fish sauce and sugar.

Transfer this mixture to the slow cooker with the pureed squash, cooking on low for 1 hour.

With around 15 minutes of cooking time remaining, stir in the cilantro and lime juice.

Serve immediately.

Tuscan Tortellini Soup

This Tuscan tortellini recipe provides a healthy and filling soup, packed full of nutrients from the fresh greens and slow-release energy from the pasta. It is a delicious lunchtime recipe that doesn't rely on the usual cream to thicken the broth and will help keep you at your best throughout the day.

Prep Time: 5-10 minutes
Cook Time: 8 hours
Serves 4

1½ cups spinach
3 asparagus, cut into 1-inch pieces 1 onion, diced
2 cloves garlic, minced
2 cups veggie broth
1 can crushed tomatoes
½ teaspoon dried basil
½ teaspoon dried oregano
Salt and pepper to taste
1 pack cheese tortellini
Grated cheese to garnish

Method

Put all the ingredients except the tortellini and cheese into the slow cooker, cook on low for 8 hours.

Add the tortellini in the last hour of cooking. Serve with grated cheese.

Cranberry Bean Soup with Fresh Greens

Cranberry beans offer a host of benefits from high-quality proteins to provide a good quantity of our bodies' iron and copper requirements. So there's no excuse for not incorporating them into a vegetarian or vegan diet.

It's a fitting option if you want a filling meal. The soup can utilize any of the spare veggies you have lying around. If you want to give it a go but don't have any cranberry beans, replace them with the likes of pinto or cannellini instead.

Prep Time: 10 minutes
Cook Time: 3.5 hours
Serves 4-6

1½ cups dried cranberry beans (sub pinto or cannellini, etc.)
6 cups water
1 vegetable bouillon cube
1 cup celery, diced
1 cup carrots, diced
½ cup onion, minced
3 cloves garlic, minced
1 tablespoon balsamic vinegar
1 teaspoon basil
1 teaspoon thyme
1 teaspoon marjoram
½ teaspoon rosemary
½ teaspoon oregano
1 can diced tomatoes
1 cup chopped greens
Salt and pepper, to taste

Method

Soak the beans overnight, drain them in the morning, and place in the slow cooker. Add everything except the tomatoes and greens, cook for 3 hours on high.

Add the tomatoes for a further 30 minutes and turn off the heat. After this, add the greens to the soup, and the heat will soften them. Serve immediately.

Side Dish Recipes

Garlicky Cauliflower Mashed Potatoes

If you're looking for a lighter alternative to mashed potato, then this recipe is your new solution. This cauliflower not only gives you the feeling that you are eating mashed potato, but it also contains a fraction of the calories and goes well with everything.

You can make it with or without garlic, but I think the addition of garlic creates a nicer texture. If you are a big garlic fan, then add up to 4 cloves. Otherwise, you can always remove the garlic prior to mashing with the bay leaf and juice.

Prep Time: 5-10 minutes
Cook Time: 2-3 hours on high/6 hours on low
Serves 5-6

2 cauliflower heads
2 garlic cloves, peeled
3 cups water1 bay leaf
1 tablespoon salt
1 tablespoon butter
Milk (optional)
Salt and pepper to season

Method

Cut the cauliflower up into more manageable florets and place in the slow cooker.

Add the garlic, water, bay leaf and salt. Cover and cook on high for 2-3 hours, alternatively, if you have the time you can cook on low for up to 6 hours.

Remove the bay leaf and drain the water. Put the butter in the cooker with the cauliflower heads, allowing it to melt and then mash or use a blender to create a creamier texture.

You can add a touch of milk to help create a creamy texture. Season to taste and serve.

Quick & Easy Refried Beans

Refried beans are an incredibly versatile side dish that is the mashed potato of Mexican cooking. If you've always opted for canned refried beans, then you're missing a treat! By cooking your own, you are adding more flavor and aromatics from the garlic, onion and spices than any premade product.

The term "refried" might not instill a healthy image, but refried beans are in fact surprisingly low in fat and contain a lot of dietary fiber and iron. Of course by cooking them yourself you can control the salt content and the exact ingredients you add, ensuring they are a healthy addition to any meal. Try having them as a side with your favorite meals or in a roast vegetable burrito.

Prep Time: 7 minutes
Cook Time: 8 hours
Serves 8

2½ cups dried pinto beans (or black beans)
1 onion, diced
3 garlic cloves, minced
1 teaspoon cumin
2 teaspoons salt
7 cups water

Method

Rinse the pinto beans and pour into the cooker. Add the diced onion, garlic, cumin and salt.

Add the water to the beans and place the lid on the cooker. Put the heat on high and cook for 8 hours.

Check the beans at the end of the cooking time; if there is any additional liquid remaining, then remove it from the cooker and set to the side.

Use either a blender or a potato masher on the beans until you achieve a smooth texture. Add some of the liquid set to the side if your beans aren't at the right consistency.

Serve as a side or add to your favorite dishes.

Cubed Butternut Squash

Naturally sweet, the squash is similar in taste and texture to sweet potato but is much lower in calories. It is an ideal addition to any meal, whether you are making sides for a BBQ or wanting to add color to a meal.

The recipe itself is a simple one and can be prepped in a matter of minutes. Once cooked, garnish with thyme to complement the flavor.

Prep Time: 5 minutes
Cook Time: 3 hours
Serves 4-6

1 butternut squash, peeled and cubed
1 tablespoon olive oil
1 teaspoon salt
1 teaspoon of brown sugar (optional)
Pepper to season
Thyme to garnish

Method

Add all the ingredients to the cooker, including the sugar if you'd like to add a little more sweetness to the squash. Give the ingredients a good mix and ensure the squash is evenly coated.

Cook on high for 3 hours and serve immediately.

Best-Ever Bombay Potatoes

Although the humble potato might not be associated with a healthy diet, it is in fact an important food source and contains a wealth of health benefits, making them an essential in any diet. Packed full of energy and nutrition, potatoes are 70-80% water. The belief you can become fat from eating them is a misconception. It is in fact the way they are cooked that can make them fatty. Be sure to give my recipe a go before you turn to the French fries. My Bombay potato recipe will ensure your potatoes are both fragrant and truly tasty. It utilizes plenty of ingredients you will have lying around the kitchen and makes for a fantastic side dish.

Prep Time: 15 minutes
Cook Time: 4 hours
Serves 4

1 teaspoon garam masala
1 teaspoon turmeric
½ teaspoon cumin
1 teaspoon dried ginger
½ teaspoon chilli powder
1 teaspoon mustard seeds
Olive oil
1 onion, finely chopped
4 tomatoes, deseeded and chopped
4 medium/large potatoes, peeled and cubed
Fresh cilantro to serve
Salt and pepper to season

Method
Combine the garam masala, turmeric, cumin, ginger and chilli powder in a bowl.

Heat the mustard seeds in a frying pan with olive oil until they begin to pop. Once they do, add the onion and gently brown. Add the bowl of mixed spices and gently heat for a few minutes. Mix in the tomatoes and potatoes until they are well covered, then place into the slow cooker and heat on low for 4 hours. You can tell the potatoes are done by piercing one with a sharp knife; if it slides in and out easily, then they are ready.

Serve the potatoes in a bowl with the cilantro as a garnish.

The Ultimate Baked Potato

Baked potatoes are a classic side and another staple for a lot of vegetarians and vegans. A simple to prepare dish, it requires little attention but is always filling and provides a lot of versatility.

The slow cooker works perfectly with baked potatoes and allows you to set them off cooking and go about your day until you're ready to eat.

Prep Time: 5 minutes
Cook Time: 7-9 hours
Serves 4-6

4-6 medium russet potatoes
4-6 teaspoons olive oil
Freshly ground sea salt and pepper
½ cup water

Method

Clean and dry the potatoes. Place each potato onto a square of aluminum foil, drizzle in oil and rub it into the skin. Sprinkle with salt and pepper, and then wrap up the potatoes in the foil.

Add the ½ cup of water to the slow cooker and add the potatoes. Cook for 7-9 hours on low until the potatoes are tender.

Serve with your preferred toppings.

Potatoes au Gratin

More of a treat and not boasting much value on the nutritional scale, potatoes au gratin is for the occasions where you crave something a little more indulgent and creamy.

This makes it perfect for special occasions, especially considering the preparation is as easy as layering the sliced potatoes and pouring on the sauce, but the result is fantastic.

The recipe can be modified to suit your particular tastes, and if you are feeling particularly indulgent then consider adding a spoon of crème fraiche.

Prep Time: 15 minutes
Cook Time: 3 hours
Serves 6-8

4 large potatoes, peeled and medium sliced
½ onion, thinly sliced
Salt and pepper to season
4 tablespoons butter
3 tablespoons plain flour
½ teaspoon minced garlic
1½ cups milk
1 cup cheddar cheese (or cheese alternative)

Method

Grease your slow cooker to ensure the gratin doesn't stick.

Place your first layer of potatoes in the bottom of the cooker and sprinkle with some of the onion.

Season well with salt and pepper. Repeat this process until either all the potatoes are used or you are happy with the number of layers.

Melt the butter in a pan and stir in the flour to create a roux. Add in the garlic and slowly whisk in the milk until you have a smooth and thick sauce. Then add in the cheese until it has melted (set some aside for the topping). You should have a rich and creamy sauce.

Pour the sauce evenly over the potatoes and add the remaining cheese on top. When placing the lid on top, a useful tip is to place paper towels on top of the slow cooker; this absorbs any moisture and ensures you have a crispier topping. You may have to change the towels occasionally, so judge accordingly.

Cook for 3 hours on high or until you are happy the potatoes are cooked and have a nice golden, crispy finish.

It's easiest to serve directly from the cooker onto plates.

Brussels Sprouts

Unfairly neglected until the festive season, brussels sprouts are a source of vitamins C and K. Foods high in vitamin C are vital for aiding in the absorption of iron, which is especially important for vegetarians and vegans, who can be at a greater risk of developing iron deficiencies.

This brussels sprout recipe is as simple as it gets, but in return you are given deliciously tasty and charred greens. Try experimenting with a teaspoon of mustard or honey to liven the recipe up even further.

Prep Time: 5 minutes
Cook Time: 2-3 hours
Serves 4-6

1 pound brussels sprouts
2 tablespoons olive oil
2 cloves garlic, peeled
¼ cup water
Salt and pepper

Method

Prepare the brussels sprouts by washing and trimming the ends, then cut in halves. Add them to the cooker with the remaining ingredients and cook on high for 2-3 hours.

Keep an eye on the sprouts throughout cooking; you want them to brown and once they do, turn them over to brown the other side as well.

Tasty Roasted Beets

Beets offer exceptional nutritional value, from the greens that are rich in calcium, iron and vitamin A, to the beets themselves that are an excellent source of folic acid and fiber. Roasting them in your slow cooker adds a lovely color, taste and texture to any dish or salad. Making them a versatile side for vegetarians.

Prep Time: 5 minutes
Cook Time: 3-4 hours
Serves 6-10

4-6 beets
4-6 teaspoons olive oil
Salt

Method

Clean any dirt off the beets, and trim the tops off.

Drizzle each beet in oil and sprinkle with salt. Wrap each of them individually in aluminum foil and place in the slow cooker.

Cover and cook on high for 3-4 hours until tender. Allow to cool, remove skins and slice to serve.

Perfect Festive Stuffing

Ideal if you're looking to make extra room in the oven for Thanksgiving, my stuffing recipe is a great vegetarian option (which can easily be made vegan) that the whole family will love, regardless of whether they're meat eaters or not.

Prep Time: 5 minutes
Cook Time: 4 hours
Serves 8

½ cup butter (or dairy-free alternative)
1 cup chopped onion
1 cup chopped celery
6 ounces sliced mushrooms
1 handful dried cranberries
⅛ cup chopped fresh parsley
½ teaspoon seasoning
1 teaspoon dried sage
½ teaspoon dried thyme
6 cups dried breadcrumbs (use fresh bread that was dried night before)
Salt and black pepper
2½ cups vegetable broth, or as needed
1 egg, beaten (or egg replacer)

Method

Melt the butter in a frying pan with the onion, celery, mushroom, parsley, stirring regularly until the onion is translucent.

In a large bowl, mix the vegetables with the seasonings, breadcrumbs, and salt and pepper. Add enough of the broth to moisten, and mix in the egg.

Transfer the mixture to the slow cooker and cook on low for 4 hours.

Zesty Lemon Broccoli

Slow cooker broccoli is a great alternative way to enjoy broccoli. Simply throw it into the cooker with the other ingredients, and enjoy this delicious side. Broccoli is a fantastic green to include in your diet and improves bone health and heart health, and alkalizes the body.

Prep Time: 5 minutes
Cook Time: 1 hour
Serves 3-4

1-2 broccoli crowns, cut into bite-size pieces
½ cup water
¼ cup white wine
1 lemon, zest and juice (as much as you like)
Salt and pepper to taste

Method

Add all the ingredients except the lemon to the slow cooker and stir. Cover and cook on high for 1 hour or until it reaches the tenderness you like.

Before serving, sprinkle the lemon zest over the broccoli and squeeze the lemon juice over it as well.

Authentic German Potato Salad

Potato salad comes in many different forms all around the world. In this recipe I've focused on the authentic German style.

This is my favorite version — of course, from a slow cooker! Enjoy this Authentic German Potato Salad any time of year! It is completely optional whether you want to add any vegan alternative to bacon, but either way, I guarantee there won't be any leftovers!

Prep Time: 10 minutes
Cook Time: 6 hours
Serves 4

4 slices vegan bacon, cooked and sliced (optional)
1 small red onion, thinly sliced
2 pounds red potatoes, cut into ¼-inch slices
3 tablespoons olive oil
⅓ cup apple cider vinegar
2 teaspoons Dijon mustard
1 tablespoon sugar
Salt and pepper to taste
3 tablespoons sliced green onion, for garnish

Method

Add the onion and potatoes to the slow cooker.

Combine the oil, vinegar, mustard and sugar in a bowl. Pour it onto the cooker's contents and coat well.

Cover and cook on low for 6 hours.

Season and garnish with fresh greens.

Beautiful Bavarian Red Cabbage

This slow-cooked Bavarian cabbage recipe is a delicious side that is full of flavor. Red cabbage is also a particularly healthy vegetable; one serving contains 56% of our recommended daily intake of vitamin C. This helps keep skin, bones and muscles healthy.

Prep Time: 5-10 minutes
Cook Time: 8-10 hours
Serves 6

1 large head of red cabbage, washed and coarsely sliced
2 onions, medium, coarsely chopped
6 apples, tart, cored and quartered
2 cup water, hot
⅔ cup vinegar, cider
3 tablespoons sugar
3 tablespoons butter (or alternative)
Salt to taste

Method

Put all the ingredients in the cooker. Cover and cook on low for 8-10 hours.

Stir and serve.

Versatile Spanish Rice

Spanish rice is a perfect side dish, providing a good deal of sustenance as well as flavor, something rice dishes don't always provide. It is an ideal companion to any Mexican food and requires very little effort.

If you'd like to be extra healthy, then try replacing the basmati rice with brown rice instead.

Prep Time: 5-10 minutes
Cook Time: 2½-3½ hours
Serves 4-6

2 cups basmati rice, uncooked (or available rice)
1 medium onion, diced
1 green bell pepper
2 cups vegetable broth
14.5 ounces tomatoes, diced
2 teaspoons chili powder
2 teaspoons cumin
1 teaspoon sea salt
Optional veggies: carrot, zucchini and etc. (chopped finely)
2 tablespoons fresh cilantro

Method

Grease the cooker, and add the rice, onion and pepper.

Combine with the rest of the ingredients (including any additional vegetables you like) except the cilantro.

Cover and cook on high for 2½ to 3½ hours. Once the rise is soft and the moisture has been absorbed, it is ready.

Creamy Mashed Potatoes

This mashed potatoes recipe makes the perfect side even easier. Often regarded as a comfort food, potatoes actually can provide a good deal of health benefits. Their vitamin C content acts as an antioxidant and can aid everything from digestion to cancer prevention. You don't even have to peel the potatoes. Instead just pop them into the slow cooker and then add the remaining ingredients before serving.

Prep Time: 5-10 minutes
Cook Time: 2-3 hours
Serves 6

2 pounds red potatoes, cut into 2-inch pieces (or however many your cooker has room for)
¼ cup almond milk
2 teaspoons minced garlic
½ cup sour cream (optional)
Salt and black pepper

Method

Add the potatoes to the slow cooker. Cover and cook on high for 2-3 hours.

Add the remaining ingredients and use a hand mixer or masher to combine.

You could even throw in some butternut squash puree for extra flavor.

Season to your liking and serve.

Ranch Potatoes

One of the easiest and tastiest recipes you can make with potatoes and the slow cooker. Ranch potatoes pack a lot of flavor and are ideal for summer salads and family BBQs — in fact they'll go with just about anything.

Prep Time: 5 minutes
Cook Time: 2-3 hours
Serves 4-6

1½ pounds potatoes, cut into bite-size pieces (gold or red)
1 tablespoon olive oil
1 tablespoon ranch seasoning
Chopped chives to garnish

Method

Line the slow cooker with aluminum foil.

Add all the ingredients to the slow cooker and mix together well. Seal the foil and cook on high for 2-3 hours, until tender.

Creamy Cauliflower Cheese

Cauliflower cheese is a delicious side that we could quite happily enjoy as a main! You can also use your slow cooker to make a big batch of it to cater to a family get-together or if you simply love leftovers. As well as tasting great, cauliflower is also a great source of fiber, vitamin C and K.

Prep Time: 10 minutes
Cook Time: 6-7 hours
Serves 4-8

1 or 2 heads of cauliflower, cut into florets
1 onion, diced
1 tablespoon olive oil
4 cloves garlic, minced
½ teaspoon paprika
1 teaspoon vegetable broth and additional water
1 teaspoon kosher salt
½ teaspoon ground black pepper
1½ cup regular almond milk
½ cup shredded Parmesan cheese (omit or replace Parmesan if desired)
2 tablespoons regular flour

Method

Add the cauliflower and onion to the slow cooker.

In a pan, heat the oil and sauté the garlic. Then add the rest of the ingredients, mix the ingredients constantly to form a creamy sauce.

Pour the sauce over the cauliflower and cook on low for 6-7 hours.

Creamed Corn

The word "cream" doesn't rule out every single meal for vegans. My creamed corn recipe is a cinch to make and is equally as sweet and tender as any other recipe you will find. It's also made in the crockpot, which means there's no watching, and the prep time is as little as 2 minutes.

Prep Time: 2-5 minutes
Cook Time: 4 hours
Serves 8

32 ounces frozen corn
1 (15 ounce) can coconut milk
¼ cup butter (or alternative)
2 tablespoons sugar
¼ teaspoon red pepper flakes
Handful flat-leaf parsley, chopped
Salt and pepper

Method

Place all the ingredients except the parsley in the cooker and cook on low for 4 hours. At the end of cooking, add in the parsley, stir, and serve.

You can also blend part of the mixture if you'd like a thicker texture and combine with the rest of the chowder.

Honey Glazed Carrots

Carrots have some fantastic health benefits but are often ignored when it comes to recipes. So instead of boiling the life out of them, why not try jazzing them up a little with my honey carrot recipe! They add a great color to any meal or buffet, and kids will love the flavor.

Prep Time: 5 minutes
Cook Time: 3 hours
Serves 6-8

1 pound baby carrots or peeled full-size carrots, sliced into bite-size pieces
1 tablespoon butter
1 tablespoon honey
1 teaspoon Dijon mustard
1-2 drops of Tabasco (optional)
Salt & pepper
Fresh cilantro, for serving

Method

Add all the ingredients except the cilantro to the slow cooker. Mix them together well and cook on high for 3 hours.

Garnish with cilantro and serve.

Winter Root Vegetables

Roasting vegetables in the slow cooker is an effortless and simple way to enjoy vegetables. Unlike roasting in the oven, you don't have to keep an eye on the veggies, and it can be left throughout the day until it's ready to serve. You're also getting the benefits of eating a good selection of root vegetables, and you can include any vegetables you like into the mix.

Prep Time: 5-10 minutes
Cook Time: 8 hours
Serves 10

2 pounds carrots, chopped
2 pounds rutabagas, peeled and chopped
2 pounds parsnips, peeled and chopped
3 tablespoons olive oil
½ cup chopped parsley
Salt and pepper

Method

Adjust the amount of vegetables you use depending on how many people you are cooking for or the amount of leftovers you would like.

Add all the vegetables to the slow cooker, cover with the oil, and season.

Cover and cook on low for 8 hours. Check tenderness before serving — you can always switch the heat setting to high towards the end of cooking.

Fresh Corn on the Cob

Cooking corn on the cob in the slow cooker is a great way to have a fun side during the summer months. It's incredibly simple and frees up space in the oven or grill for other food. A rich source of vitamins A, B and E, corn's antioxidant activity has been reported to actually increase when cooked.

Prep Time: 5 minutes
Cook Time: 4-5 hours
Serves 4-5

4-5 fresh corn
Water
Pinch of salt

Method

Place shucked corn on the cob in the crockpot and fill with water, adding the salt as well.

Cover and cook on high for 4-5 hours.

Once cooked, remove from the cooker and serve with butter or spices.

Simple & Tasty Vegan Stuffing

A variation of my festive stuffing, nothing says warm and wholesome quite like stuffing. It is a satisfying addition to any type of roast, and this recipe will have even meat eaters coming back for more. This is a healthy side dish, full of nutrients from the veggies and lots of flavor.

Prep Time: 10 minutes
Cook Time: 4-5 hours
Serves 8

2 onions, chopped
2 cups celery, chopped
3-4 mushrooms, sliced
¼ cup chopped fresh parsley
3½–4 cups veggie broth, divided
10-12 cups whole wheat or cornbread bread crumbs
1½ teaspoons sage
1 teaspoon poultry seasoning
½ teaspoon marjoram
1 teaspoon dried thyme
½ teaspoon ground black pepper
Salt to taste

Method

Begin by sautéing the onions, celery, mushrooms and parsley in a little of the veggie broth.

Add this mixture into a mixing bowl with the breadcrumbs and all the seasonings. Mix together and then pour in some of the broth to moisten the mixture.

Pack the stuffing into the slow cooker and cover. Cook on the high setting for 45 minutes, and then reduce to low for 3-4 hours. Check the mixture every so often and add extra broth for a moister result.

Potato Stuffed Cabbage

A fun and creative way to cook a classic side, potato stuffed cabbage has a low calorie count and is a tasty way to get a good dose of vitamin C. For more of an indulgent treat, try adding a scoop of ricotta.

Prep Time: 15-20 minutes
Cook Time: 4 hours
Serves 4-6

1 head cabbage
5 pounds potatoes, peeled
2 onions, diced, divided
1 teaspoon dill
2 tablespoon butter, melted
1 apple, peeled and sliced
¼ teaspoon ground ginger
1 can tomatoes

Method

Parboil the cabbage and then separate the leaves. Remove any thick stalks.

Grate the potatoes, the smaller inner leaves of the cabbage and mix with half the onions, dill and melted butter.

Add this mixture evenly into the large cabbage leaves. Fold the leaves inwards, around the mixture, and roll up. If the cabbage roll doesn't hold, then secure with a toothpick.

Use the remaining leaves to line the bottom of the slow cooker, placing the second half of onion, apple, ginger and tomato on top of the leaves. Line the stuffed cabbage rolls on top, and cook on a low heat for 4 hours.

Acorn Squash with Orange-Cranberry Sauce

A perfect accompaniment to any salad or roast, this acorn squash with orange-cranberry sauce is a fresh and mouth-watering side. Acorn squash is a nutrient-dense vegetable that any vegetarian should be looking to introduce into their diet. It has the ability to boost the immune system, protect the skin, improve vision and much more.

Prep Time: 10 minutes
Cook Time: 6-7 hours
Serves 4-6

2 medium acorn squash
1 jar cranberry sauce
¼ cup orange marmalade
¼ cup raisins
Pinch of ground cinnamon
Salt and pepper

Method

Cut the squash into 1-inch thick slices. Arrange flesh up in the slow cooker.

Combine the other ingredients in a small pan and heat gently until smooth. Pour the sauce over the squash.

Cover and cook on low for 6-7 hours.

Warm Eggplant and Kale Panzanella

For an alternative take on a salad why not try this warm eggplant and kale panzanella? It is perfect for warmer weather, and the bread cubes soak up all the delicious juices from the fresh ingredients. Be as rustic as you like when cutting the veggies. I love nice chunky pieces.

Prep Time: 15 minutes
Cook Time: 2 hours
Serves 6

4 cups eggplant, chopped
1 can diced fire-roasted tomatoes
1 yellow sweet pepper, chopped
1 red onion, cut into wedges
2 cups kale, chopped
2 tablespoons olive oil
3 tablespoons red wine vinegar
1 clove garlic, minced
Black pepper
Squeeze of lemon juice
Fresh basil
4 cups good quality crusty bread, toasted
Parmesan cheese (optional)

Method

Place the eggplant, tomatoes, pepper and onion in the slow cooker. Cover and cook for 2 hours on high. Add in the kale and cook for a further 15 minutes.

Mix the olive oil, red wine vinegar, lemon juice, garlic and black pepper in a bowl.

Drain the vegetables from the slow cooker before transferring to a bowl. Add the dressing, basil and bread. Gently combine all the ingredients and sprinkle with basil and cheese (optional).

Barley-Squash Gratin

A creamy, sweet and comforting dish, this is ideal served as either a side or in a larger portion as a main. The plump pearl barley perfectly complements the pieces of butternut squash and is also a nutritional powerhouse, packed full of fiber, nutrients, antioxidants and phytochemicals.

Prep Time: 10-15 minutes
Cook Time: 3-3½ hours
Serves 12 as a side/6 as a main

4-5 cups butternut squash, peeled and cubed
10-ounce package frozen chopped spinach, thawed and well drained
1 medium onion, cut into wedges
1 cup regular barley (not quick-cooking)
3 cloves garlic, minced
1½ cups vegetable broth
½ cup water
¾ teaspoon salt
¼ teaspoon ground black pepper
½ cup shredded Parmesan cheese (or similar alternative)

Method

Add all the ingredients except the cheese to the slow cooker. Cover and cook on high for 3-3½ hours.

Once cooked, turn off the heat and sprinkle on the Parmesan. Let it work its magic for 10 minutes, then serve.

Orange-Sage Sweet Potatoes with Tofu Bacon

Bring a little life to your usual sweet potatoes with this herb-accented and zesty recipe. Sweet potatoes are a vegetarian's best friend but are often neglected when it comes to recipes, so why not treat yourself to something a little different that will help enhance their natural flavors even further.

Prep Time: 10-15 minutes
Cook Time: 2½-3 hours on high or 5-6 hours on low
Serves 6

1 bag sweet potatoes, peeled and cut into slices
½ cup orange juice
3 tablespoons brown sugar
½ teaspoon dried sage
½ teaspoon dried thyme
2 tablespoons butter
2-4 slices tofu bacon, crisp-cooked and chopped
Salt and pepper, to taste

Method

Place the sweet potatoes in the slow cooker. Combine the orange juice and seasoning in a small bowl. Pour the mixture over the sweet potatoes and coat well. Add the butter.

Cover and cook on low for 5-6 hours or on high for 2½-3 hours.

Once cooked, mix to cover with the sauce and serve with sprinkled tofu bacon.

Butternut Squash Frijoles

The perfect recipe for fans of spicy Mexican food, these refried beans incorporate butternut squash to fantastic effect. They not only provide additional sweetness and flavor but also plenty of nutrition. The cilantro and lime give it freshness, and you can add as much heat as you want from the chipotle.

Prep Time: 10 minutes
Cook Time: 7-8 hours on low
Serves 4-6

1 cup dried beans (anasazi, pinto or other brown beans)
3 cups water
1 cup butternut squash purée
1 clove garlic, minced
1 can diced tomatoes
1 teaspoon marjoram
½ teaspoon chili powder
1 tablespoon fresh cilantro, chopped
½ teaspoon powdered chipotle
Juice of ½ lime
Salt to taste

Method

Add the dried beans and water to the slow cooker and cook on low overnight (up to 8 hours).

In the morning, put the squash, garlic, tomato, marjoram and chili powder in with the beans. Mix and let it sit.

Taste and adjust the seasoning, adding the cilantro and chipotle, to your preference.

Drizzle the lime juice over the frijoles, and serve.

Tender and Flavorful Bok Choy

A cup of bok choy has as little as 9 calories but delivers a healthy dose of protein, dietary fiber and essential vitamins — making this vegetable a nutrient-dense food and a welcoming side. Here we simmer the bok choy slowly in a delicious sauce for a tender and flavorful dish.

Prep Time: 5-10 minutes
Cook Time: 4 hours
Serves 3-4

2 tablespoons soy sauce
1 tablespoon hoisin sauce
1 tablespoon mirin
1 tablespoon water
1 tablespoon peanut oil
1 large garlic clove, minced
1 teaspoon ginger, peeled and minced
2-3 heads baby bok choy, trimmed and halved lengthwise
3 scallions, thinly sliced

Method

Mix the soy sauce, hoisin, mirin and water in a bowl. Set aside.

Add oil to the slow cooker and turn to high. Add the garlic and ginger, then the bok choy. Add the scallions on top, then drizzle over the sauce.

Turn the heat to low, cover and cook for 4 hours or until you notice the bok choy are tender, and serve.

Wild Rice Medley

Rich in complex carbohydrates and protein, wild rice is natural side or could even serve as a main meal that will give you the energy to be at your best throughout the day. Its slow cooking time also lends itself perfectly to the slow cooker as you can happily leave it unattended.

Prep Time: 5 minutes
Cook Time: 4 hours
Serves 2-4

1 cup wild rice
1 medium onion, diced
1 large carrot, diced
1 stalk celery, diced
2½ cups vegetable broth
2 cloves garlic, minced
2 tablespoons dried porcini
½ teaspoon dried chervil
Black pepper

Method

Add all the ingredients to the cooker and combine. Cover and cook on low heat for 4 hours. Check to see whether the kernels are tender. If not, then continue cooking, checking regularly to avoid overcooking.

Dessert Recipes

Warming Peach cobbler

If you're after a simple yet delicious dessert, then look no further than this peach cobbler. Slow cookers have always been go-to tools for creating cobblers, providing the perfect combination of deeply flavorful fruit and a crispy yet soft biscuit-like topping.

Cobblers are an incredibly popular dessert thanks to their quick preparation time and the great pay-off you get in return. You can use either fresh or frozen peaches, but I prefer to keep it fresh. Struggling to find peaches? Why not try replacing them with seasonal fruit instead. Finish with your choice of topping, from ice cream to whipped coconut cream.

Prep Time: 10 minutes
Cook Time: 3 hours
Serves 4-6

½ cup dark brown sugar
4 ounces all-purpose flour
3½ ounces rolled oats
½ teaspoon grated nutmeg
½ teaspoon baking powder
Pinch of salt
¼ cup unsalted butter, at room temperature
4 cups fresh or frozen sliced peaches
Ice cream or whipped cream, to serve

Method

Combine the sugar, flour, oats, nutmeg, baking powder and salt in a bowl. Work the butter into the dry ingredients to create a crumble.

Once the mixture clings to itself, place the peaches in the bottom of the slow cooker and cover with the mixture. Note the mixture doesn't have to entirely cover the peaches; I love to create a more sparse and rustic feel.

Cook on low for 3 hours and then serve with your favorite topping.

Luxurious Coconut Hot Chocolate

Hot chocolate might not usually win too many awards for the most nutritious drink, but if you're after a warming and luxurious drink free from dairy, then my coconut hot chocolate is the perfect solution. Thankfully coconut provides us with plenty of good fats, and the addition of high-quality dark chocolate will provide antioxidants. Both these ingredients are also responsible for creating a rich and creamy texture, while the dark chocolate and cacao provide a slight bitterness.

The recipe can be customized to suit your personal preferences, whether you prefer a little more sweetness or even want to add a few extras, such as a dash of peppermint or even cayenne. If you're feeling particularly indulgent, then top with coconut whipped cream and marshmallows.

Prep Time: 5 minutes
Cook Time: 2 hours
Serves 4

4 cans full-fat coconut milk
1 can cream of coconut
2 teaspoons vanilla extract
8 ounces dark chocolate, chopped
¼ cup cocoa powder
¼ teaspoon salt
Coconut whipped cream (optional)
Marshmallows (optional)

Method

Mix the coconut milk, cream of coconut and extract in your slow cooker. Add the chocolate, cocoa powder and salt, stirring in all the ingredients.

Cover the mixture and cook on low for 2 hours. Check the cooker regularly to ensure the chocolate has melted and that the contents remain well mixed.

Serve the coconut hot chocolate in your favorite mug, and if you're feeling particularly indulgent, whip up some coconut cream and add marshmallows as a topping.

Seasonal Spiced Pumpkin Butter

If you're a fan of making your own spreads, then this spiced pumpkin butter recipe will impress. All you need to do is add all the ingredients into the slow cooker and let it work its magic.

The result is a rich and creamy butter that will feel as though you are spreading pumpkin pie (minus the crust) over your bread. The spices, lemon juice and ginger provide the butter with warmth and a kick that you'll love.

Ideal for breakfasts or desserts, the butter can be put on anything from bread, to oatmeal or pancakes.

I've opted for canned pumpkin to save time, but you can puree your own pumpkin if you prefer.

Prep Time: 5 minutes
Cook Time: 3 hours
Serves 5-6

2 (15 ounce) cans pumpkin puree
½ cup apple juice
½ juiced lemon
1 cup maple syrup or honey
2 teaspoons ground ginger
½ teaspoon nutmeg
½ teaspoon cinnamon
Pinch of salt

Method

Add all the ingredients to the cooker and combine with a wooden spoon. Set the heat to low and cook for 3 hours or until you see the mixture thicken.

Once cooked, allow the butter to cool and then store it in jars. The butter will remain fresh for up to a week. Alternatively you can freeze it for up to 6 months.

Slow Cooker Apple Cider

Slow cookers aren't just for stews and soups, you can also make some fantastic warm drinks with them as well. This homemade apple cider recipe is guaranteed to fill your home with an aroma of fall and is ideal at Thanksgiving. Made entirely from scratch, you'll be getting all the benefits of using fresh apples and oranges. Be as creative as you like with apple varieties, experimenting with different colors and flavors. This can result in noticeable changes in the sweetness and crispness of your cider. This recipe is incredibly simple and requires only a handful of ingredients. It also provides you with complete control over whether you add any sugar, which often isn't necessary thanks to the natural sweetness of the apples.

Prep Time: 5 minutes
Cook Time: High for 2-3 hours/low for 8 hours
Serves 4-6

8 medium apples (try an assortment)
1 orange
½ a whole nutmeg
2 cinnamon sticks
½ teaspoon allspice
12 cups water
Brown sugar or preferred sweetener to taste

Method

Wash the apples and cut the orange into quarters (there's no need to remove cores or seeds). Add them to your slow cooker with the remaining ingredients except the water and sugar. Cover these with water; you add water until the cooker is nearly full.

Depending on how much time you have, you can either cook the contents on low for up to 8 hours or on high for 2-3 hours. Here's the fun bit: An hour before the cider is finished cooking, use a masher or fork to break down the apples and orange; this will help release more of the flavor.

Once cooked, strain the contents either by using a sieve or cheesecloth to ensure none of the juice goes to waste. Dissolve in your sweetener of choice until you are happy with the taste. Serve warm.

Merry Mulled Wine

If you love filling your home with delicious aromas during the colder months, then mulled wine is a fantastic way to do so. Of course you'll also be rewarded with a wonderful and warming drink that friends and family will keep coming back for.

Using a slow cooker makes it incredibly simple and hassle free. Rather than opting for store-bought mulled wine, take a little time to make your own and the difference in quality will be unquestionable.

Remember the quality of the wine is always important in the overall taste, but you can experiment with different spices and flavors to suit your tastes.

Prep Time: 10 minutes
Cook Time: 40 minutes
Serves 6

2 clementines
½ lemon
½ cup sugar
1 bottle red wine
2 cinnamon sticks
2 star anise
½ vanilla pod, cut open
Grated nutmeg

Method

Peel and juice the clementines and lemon, adding to the cooker along with some of their peel as well. Add the sugar and enough of the wine to cover it, heat on high. The idea is to dissolve the sugar into a syrup and by doing this at the beginning we protect the alcohol content of the rest of the wine.

Add the rest of the ingredients and stir, grating in as much nutmeg as you like. Once the mixture has come to a simmer, lower to the "keep warm" setting and let it rest for 30 minutes.

To serve, either pour straight into glasses or through a sieve if you don't want any bits.

Rich & Creamy Rice Pudding

Rice pudding is one of the most old-fashioned dessert recipes, but it still remains popular thanks to its minimal use of ingredients and comforting feel.

Scented with vanilla, it is a satisfying and tasty dessert that utilizes the many ingredients hidden away in your cupboard. Almond milk gives a lower fat and dairy-free dessert that is perfect when topped with healthy fruits and protein-rich nuts.

Prep Time: 5 minutes
Cook Time: 3-4 hours
Serves 8

¾ cup pudding rice (you can experiment with basmati and other rice)
4 cups almond milk
½ vanilla pod, cut open
Teaspoon of lemon zest (optional)
Pinch of nutmeg

Method

Add all the ingredients except the nutmeg, and cook on a low heat for 3-4 hours.

The trick lies in finding the ingredients that work for you. Feel free to replace the type of rice and milk used (coconut milk will work just as well).

Once cooked, garnish with nutmeg and serve.

Beetroot Surprise Chocolate Cake

Where once we wouldn't have dreamed of adding beets to a cake, they have now been widely accepted as a perfect combination with chocolate. Let's face it: it's also a great way to get the kids eating healthier without them even knowing about it.

Beetroot is in fact quite sweet as well as having earthy flavors; by using it we are giving the cake a rich, fudgy texture. It is also regarded as something of a superfood due to studies that claim it can lower blood pressure and improve blood flow.

This could be the healthiest cake you've ever baked and by using a slow cooker, the simplest one as well.

Prep Time: 20 minutes
Cook Time: 2½ hours
Serves 8-10

Cake:
5 ounces cooked beetroot
¾ cup sugar
1 tablespoon vanilla extract
½ cup unsalted butter, melted
3 eggs (or egg substitute)
1 cup cocoa powder
1¼ cups plain flour
2 tablespoons baking powder
½ tablespoon salt

Vanilla topping:
½ cup double cream (or coconut cream)
2 tablespoon sugar
½ teaspoon vanilla extract
1 tablespoon beetroot juice (optional)

Method

Line the cooker with baking paper and grease to ensure the cake can easily be removed.

Puree the beetroot, and then mix together with the sugar, vanilla and cooled butter. Slowly add the eggs (or replacement), and stir in well.

Mix the dry ingredients in a separate bowl, ensuring there are no lumps, and then pour into the wet mixture. Stir to combine, but do not overwork the mixture.

Add the mixture to the slow cooker and spread the batter evenly to all the edges. Pop the lid on and cook on low for 2½ hours. Allow the cake to cool a while before attempting to remove it.

While it cools, make the vanilla topping. Whip the cream and sugar together until it thickens. Add the vanilla extract and beetroot juice, whipping again until the color is consistent. Spread over the cake once it has completely cooled.

Dairy-Free & Decadent Chocolate Fudge Cake

If you're after the perfect guilt-free or at least dairy-free treat, then this chocolate fudge cake will be right up your street. The cake consists of 2 self-created layers — one the rich gooey bottom layer and the other a cake top. Trust us, this cake looks and tastes amazing!

I do advise you keep an eye on this recipe the first time you make it as all slow cookers can heat differently. Make sure you test it in the middle to check if it's done.

Prep Time: 15 minutes
Cook Time: 2½-3½ hours
Serves 6-8

Mixture 1:
1 cup all-purpose flour
½ cup white sugar
¼ cup brown sugar, granulated
½ teaspoon salt
¼ cup cocoa powder
½ cup almond milk
1 egg (or egg replacer)
¼ cup vegetable oil
1 teaspoon vanilla extract
80 grams dark chocolate, chopped

Mixture 2:
1¼ cup boiling water
¼ cup cocoa powder
¼ cup white sugar
¼ teaspoon salt
1½ teaspoons coffee granules, instant

Method

In a large bowl, whisk the flour, sugars, salt and cocoa. Add the milk, egg, oil and vanilla. Whisk well.

Grease the slow cooker. Add the chopped chocolate, and place mixture 1 in the slow cooker.

Mix the boiling water, cocoa, coffee, sugar and salt in bowl with a spout. Gently pour it over the mixture in the slow cooker, and don't stir.

Cover and cook on low for 2½-3½ hours. Use a kitchen towel under the lid if too much condensation forms.

Check the cake after 2 hours and judge how much longer it needs. Once cooked, allow it to cool thoroughly. This gives the cake the opportunity to soak up any remaining mixture, creating the fudgy layer.

Candied Cinnamon Almonds

These candied almonds have an irresistible aroma and they taste amazing too. They're an ideal snack when you're craving a sugary treat but need help controlling blood-sugar levels. They're also packed full of protein and antioxidants, which makes them a fitting healthy snack when you're on the move.

Prep Time: 5 minutes
Cook Time: 2½ hours
Serves 5 cups

2 egg whites (or alternative, such as honey)
2 teaspoons vanilla
5 cups dry roasted almonds
1½ cups white sugar
1½ cups brown sugar
3 tablespoons cinnamon
⅛ teaspoon salt

Method

Beat the egg whites in a bowl until foamy. Add the vanilla and fold in the almonds until they are coated.

In a separate bowl, combine the sugars, cinnamon and salt. Pour this mixture onto the almonds. Add the almonds to the slow cooker and cook on high for 2½ hours.

Once cooked, place the almonds on a piece of parchment paper and allow to cool. Store in an airtight container.

Fudgy & Gooey Nutella Brownie

This Nutella brownie is a particularly rich and intense treat. It's definitely not winning too many nutritional awards and isn't for everyday consumption, but the brownie will be a welcoming addition to birthday parties and can even double up as a great alternative to birthday cake. The slow cooker takes all of the work out of creating this chocolate masterpiece, and you might even surprise yourself with how good it tastes!

Prep Time: 15 minutes
Cook Time: 2-3 hours
Serves 6

3 eggs (or egg replacer)
1 cup + 3 tablespoons white sugar
1 teaspoon vanilla
½ cup cocoa powder
⅓ cup all purpose flour
¼ teaspoon salt
10 tablespoons unsalted butter, melted (or alternative)
¼ cup Nutella

Method

Lightly grease an oven dish that fits inside your slow cooker, and fill the cooker with around 2 inches of water.

Use an electric mixer or whisk to beat the eggs and sugar for 5-7 minutes until very thick. Add the vanilla, cocoa, flour and salt to the mix, stirring on a low speed. Slowly add in the butter and Nutella, mixing until completely combined.

Scrape all the mixture into the prepared dish and spread evenly.

Place the dish in the slow cooker (the water should reach half way up the dish) and then secure a few thick paper towels under the lid to prevent condensation. Cook on high for 2-3 hours.

The mixture may still look moist but will be completely cooked, and will firm up once allowed to cool. Unplug the slow cooker and allow the mixture to sit for 10 minutes, then serve.

The Ultimate Slow Cooker Carrot Cake

Carrot cake is an all-time favorite of mine, and the slow cooker is a perfect environment to create a moist and perfectly cooked cake. The cream cheese frosting is entirely optional but I do love it! It can of course be subbed out with a vegan alternative of your choosing.

Prep Time: 15 minutes
Cook Time: 3-4 hours
Serves 8

Cake:
⅔ cup flour
½ cup sugar
1 teaspoon baking soda
¾ teaspoon baking powder
1 teaspoon ground cinnamon
¼ teaspoon ground nutmeg
1 teaspoon freshly grated ginger
¼ teaspoon salt
⅓ cup vegetable oil
2 eggs (or egg replacer)
1 (8 ounce) can of crushed pineapple with juice
½ cup golden raisins
1 cup pecans or walnuts, chopped (optional)
1 cup finely grated carrot

Frosting:
4 ounces cream cheese, softened (or alternative)
1 cup powdered sugar
½ teaspoon vanilla extract

Method

Start with the cake. Combine the flour, sugar, baking soda, baking powder, cinnamon, nutmeg, ginger and salt in a bowl.

In a separate bowl, mix the oil, eggs, pineapple, raisins, nuts and carrot.

Add the dry and wet ingredients together, mixing by hand to thoroughly combine.

Grease a loaf pan or cake tin that fits into your slow cooker. Pour the cake mixture into the pan and place in the slow cooker.

Cover the top of the slow cooker with paper towels, cover with the lid and cook on high for 3-4 hours.

Once cooked, allow the cake to cool for 5 minutes then invert the cake onto the cooling rack and let it cool completely before frosting.

For the frosting, whip the cream cheese until fluffy, add the sugar and vanilla. Spread on the cake and serve.

Caramel Baked Apples

Baked apples provide all the great flavor of an apple pie without the crust. That means you can enjoy a dessert with far fewer calories and no compromise on taste. Throw in chopped walnuts to provide lots of nutrients, and you'll have a dessert that ticks all the right boxes.

Prep Time: 10 minutes
Cook Time: 2½-3 hours
Serves 4-6

¼ cup brown sugar
¼ cup walnuts, chopped
2 tablespoons butter (or alternative)
1 teaspoon cinnamon
6 Gala or Macintosh apples, cored
½ cup apple juice or apple cider
2 tablespoons orange liqueur (optional)

Method

Mix the brown sugar, walnuts, butter and cinnamon in a bowl. (You can use practically any nuts you like or even a mixture.)

Remove most of the core from each apple, leaving around ½ inch of apple at the base for the mixture to sit in. Fill the apples with the mixture and place in the slow cooker.

Pour the apple juice into the crockpot, set the heat to high, and cook for 2½-3 hours.

Serve with your choice of yogurt or ice cream.

Chocolaty Peanut Butter Balls

These chocolate peanut butter balls are a fantastic treat, consisting of my favorite ingredients! It's a simple recipe and a relatively healthy way to sate any sugar cravings. The peanut butter is packed full of protein and helps to suppress hunger, making it ideal for between meals.

Prep Time: 1 hour (including freezing time), 20 minutes
Cook Time: 1 hour
Serves many

½ cup peanut butter (smooth or chunky)
⅓ cup butter, melted (or dairy-free alternative)
⅛ teaspoon vanilla
1 cup shredded coconut and more to sprinkle on top
1 cup powdered sugar
½ cup rice krispies
½ pound chocolate

Method

Mix the peanut butter, butter, vanilla, coconut, sugar and rice krispies in a bowl. Stir until smooth.

Use a tablespoon to shape balls of the mixture. Place them on a cookie sheet covered by parchment paper. Freeze for 1 hour.

Add the chocolate to the slow cooker, cover and heat on low for 1 hour. Stir the chocolate occasionally until it becomes creamy.

Dip the dough balls into the chocolate using a fork. Cover the balls entirely and place back onto the parchment paper.

Sprinkle with coconut as a finishing touch.

The Perfect Pumpkin Cheesecake

A perfect alternative to pumpkin pie, anyone who is a fan of cheesecake will love this recipe! I've used canned pumpkin, but if you prefer, you can puree your own pumpkin — it'll just need a bit more work. Did I mention that a slice of this cheesecake is also a great source of vitamin B and healthy minerals? I love it when we can sneak a little bit of good into a dessert.

Prep Time: 20 minutes
Cook Time: 2-2½ hours
Serves 8

3 (8 ounce) packages of Philadelphia cream cheese, at room temperature
¾ cup sugar
3 eggs (or egg replacer)
1 teaspoon pumpkin pie spice (or ½ teaspoon ground cinnamon, ⅛ teaspoon ground nutmeg, ⅛ teaspoon ground cloves)
1 can (15 ounce) pumpkin (not pumpkin pie mix)
1 teaspoon vanilla
1 cup gingersnap cookies or graham crackers, crushed
4 tablespoons butter, melted
1½ tablespoons brown sugar
3 cups water

Method
Mix the cream cheese and sugar in a bowl. Add one egg at a time, mixing well each time. Add the pumpkin spices, pumpkin and vanilla. Mix well.

For the crust, combine the cookies or crackers with the melted butter and brown sugar. Stir until combined. Press the cracker mixture into the bottom of a greased pan that can fit inside your slow cooker. Transfer the filling into the pan on top of the crust.

Put around 3 cups of water into the slow cooker and rest the cheesecake pan in it. Make sure the water doesn't come too high on the tin (no more than ⅔ of the way up).

Cover and cook on high for 2-2½ hours. Continue to cook until the center of the cheesecake is cooked. Turn the slow cooker off, allowing the cheesecake to cool. Remove and refrigerate.

Pumpkin Custard

Essentially a pumpkin pie without the crust, pumpkin custard makes for a perfect dessert or breakfast. Rich in beta-carotene and antioxidants, pumpkin has many health benefits and will also keep you feeling full thanks to its high fiber content.

Prep Time: 70 minutes (not including cooking pumpkin)
Cook Time: 4-6 hours
Serves 5 cups

3 cups cooked pumpkin (could sub with pumpkin puree)
6 eggs
¼ cup coconut milk, full fat
¼ cup maple syrup or honey
½ teaspoon ginger
½ teaspoon cinnamon
Pinch of sea salt

Method

Fill the slow cooker with 1 inch of water and turn heat setting to high. Pre-heat the cooker for at least 30 minutes.

Puree all the ingredients in a blender. Pour the mixture into heatproof ramekins and place in the slow cooker. It is fine to stack the ramekins if you have a smaller slow cooker.

Cook for 4-6 hours, depending on how fast your cooker heats, and serve immediately.

Zingy Orange Cheesecake

If you thought your slow cooker dessert options were limited to cobblers and rice pudding, then you're sorely mistaken. This cheesecake recipe is not only simple to make but it is also wonderfully light, so you can enjoy a tasty dessert without feeling weighed down.

Prep Time: 15 minutes, plus chilling time
Cook Time: 3 hours
Serves 6-8

Crust:
6 graham crackers (whole)
Non-stick cooking spray
Filling:
¾ cup water
3 tablespoons cornstarch
8 ounces tofu (regular)
8 ounces cream cheese
⅔ cup sugar
2 tablespoons brown sugar
1 teaspoon vanilla extract
1 medium orange, juiced and zested

Method
Fill the slow cooker with ½-inch of water and place an upside-down bowl or trivet in the cooker. Place the lid on and turn heat to high.

Pulse the crackers in a food processor. Grease a round cake pan with the cooking spray and place the crumbs into the bottom of the pan, spreading them evenly across the base.

For the filling, mix the water and cornstarch in a blender jar. Then add the rest of the filling ingredients except the orange. Blend the contents until they become creamy. Once at the right texture, add the orange juice and zest, gently stir in.

Add the filling on top of the graham cracker base. Place the cake tin onto the trivet inside the slow cooker, cover and cook for 3 hours on high. Once cooked, turn off the heat, remove the lid and allow the cake to cool before refrigerating for a few hours and serving.

Decadent Chocolate Rice Mousse

If you're after a simple and wholesome dessert, then my chocolate rice mousse is going to match your yearnings. Utilizing only a handful of ingredients, all you have to do is throw them in your slow cooker and then cool in the fridge to have a thick and glorious mousse waiting for you.

Did I mention that out of all rice, only black rice contains anthocyanin? Which improves health and helps ward off disease.

Prep Time: 5 minutes, plus chilling time
Cook Time: 2½-3 hours
Serves 4-6

1 (14 ounce) can full fat coconut milk
¼ cup forbidden rice (use less to make pudding instead of mousse)
½ cup chocolate chips (milk or dark)
1 teaspoon vanilla

Method

Add all the ingredients to your slow cooker and cook on high for 2½-3 hours. The mixture will look runny and the rice will have a natural bite to it, but put the mixture in the fridge for at least 5 hours and it will firm up nicely.

Vegan Creamsicle Tapioca Pudding

Traditional tapioca puddings require a lot of attention, but by using a slow cooker you get the same results with minimal effort. This recipe utilizes coconut milk as well as a hint of orange and vanilla for a perfect vegan dessert.

This recipe can be doubled if you want to make a large batch or have a large slow cooker.

Prep Time: 2 minutes, plus chilling time
Cook Time: 3½-4 hours
Serves 2-4

½ cup small pearl tapioca
1 container coconut milk
2 teaspoons orange extract
1 teaspoon vanilla extract
Sweetener, such as agave or stevia (optional)
Fresh berries, to serve
Fresh mint, to serve

Method

Place all the ingredients in the slow cooker. Cook on low for 3½-4 hours.

Cooking time may vary depending on your slow cooker, so keep an eye out every once in a while. Remember that the pudding won't set completely in the cooker, only after leaving it in the fridge for a few hours.

Serve with fresh berries and a sprig of mint.

Spongy Blueberry Lemon Cake

A slow cooker is the ideal method of cooking cakes, and the moist and sumptuous Spongy Blueberry Lemon Cake is the perfect example of it. If you are yet to try making a cake in your cooker, then this is one of the simplest and most rewarding recipes. Just remember to place a clean dishtowel under the lid to soak up any moisture and ensure your cake bakes perfectly.

Prep Time: 10 minutes
Cook Time: 1-1.2 hours
Serves 6

Dry ingredients:
½ cup whole-wheat pastry flour
¼ teaspoon baking powder
¼ teaspoon stevia
1 teaspoon agave or sweetener of your choice

Wet ingredients:
⅓ cup (80 ml) unsweetened almond milk
¼ cup blueberries
1 teaspoon ground flax seeds mixed with 2 teaspoons warm water
1 teaspoon olive oil or applesauce
½ teaspoon lemon zest
¼ teaspoon lemon extract
¼ teaspoon vanilla extract

Method

Line the cooker with parchment paper.

Mix the dry ingredients in a bowl and the wet ingredients in another. Then add the two together and mix until combined.

Power the mixture into the parchment. Remember to place a towel between the lid and cooker to remove condensation.

Cook on high for 1 hour to 1 hour 20 minutes. Test the center by touch (when ready, there should be no indent after pressing).

Allow to cool on a cooling tray.

Pumpkin Spice Latte

If you love the taste of pumpkin spice in your latte, then you should definitely consider making your own. This easy-to-make syrup is perfect for adding to coffee drinks and drizzling over pancakes or ice cream.

Prep Time: 5 minutes
Cook Time: 7-9 hours
Serves 2

1 cup organic pumpkin puree
1 can full-fat coconut milk
1 cup packed light brown sugar
½ teaspoon ground cinnamon
½ teaspoon ground ginger
⅛ teaspoon ground cardamom
⅛ teaspoon ground allspice

Method

Add all the ingredients to the slow cooker. Mix together well and cook on low for 7-9 hours or overnight.

Once cooker, whisk the contents to remove any clumps and store in the refrigerator for up to a week.

Amazing Apple Crisp Pudding

Apple crisp is an easy-to-make dessert that is perfect served warm or even cold the next day. The differing textures of the apples and the crisp topping perfectly complement each other and are ideal served with a scoop of ice cream.

For an easy dessert the whole family will love, you need look no further.

Prep Time: 10 minutes
Cook Time: 4 hours
Serves 6

6 cups apples, chopped (mixed varieties)
2 tablespoons lemon juice
1 tablespoon apple butter
1 tablespoon cornstarch
¼ cup white sugar
2 tablespoons apple pie spice, divided
¼ cup chopped walnuts (optional)
¾ cup all-purpose flour
¾ cup packed brown sugar
Pinch of salt
4½ tablespoons butter
Ice cream to serve

Method

Place the apples in the bottom of the slow cooker. Add the lemon juice and apple butter, coating the apples in the mixture.

Mix the cornstarch, white sugar and half the apple pie spice. Add the mixture to the apples and mix well. Add the walnuts if using.

In a bowl, mix the flour, brown sugar, remaining apple spice and salt. Add the butter and mix until it forms a crumbly texture. Sprinkle over the apples and cover.

Cook on low for 4 hours. Serve warm.

Mouth-watering Coconut Chocolate Fudge

When you're having a sugar craving, this coconut chocolate fudge is a dairy-free and almost guilt-free treat. The fudge is particularly rich and creamy. Made with coconut butter, raw honey and cocoa powder, using your slow cooker makes it all too easy.

Prep Time: 15 minutes, plus chilling time
Cook Time: 2 hours
Serves 4

1½ cups coconut butter
½ cup cocoa powder
½ cup raw honey or natural sweetener of choice
1 tablespoon vanilla extract
A pinch of sea salt (optional)

Method

Add all the ingredients except the vanilla and salt to the slow cooker and stir to combine. Cover and cook on low for 2 hours.

After 2 hours, pour on the vanilla extract but don't stir the mixture! Allow the mixture to cool to room temperature, then stir vigorously for 5 minutes and pour into a lightly greased square pan. Cover and refrigerate for 4 hours.

Sprinkle with salt if desired, and cut into squares. Store in an airtight container.

Kitchen Staple Recipes

Whole-Cooked Butternut Squash

Butternut squash is a perfect staple for vegetarian and vegan diets. An alternative to potato, butternut squash is a low fat vegetable that is packed full of dietary fiber, providing you with a tasty and heart-friendly side. In fact, one cup of squash provides you with 437% of your vitamin A needs for the day and even provides more potassium than a banana. There's plenty of benefit in eating it regularly.

This staple can be utilized in a wide variety of ways, from mixing into pasta or adding to hummus. I love to cook one or two at the start of every week. Regardless of what you use it for, cooking a whole butternut squash in the slow cooker provides you with a convenient and versatile option that you can refrigerate for days.

Prep Time: 1 minute
Cook Time: 4-5 hours on high

Ingredients

1 whole butternut squash, washed

Method

Simply place the whole squash in the slow cooker and cook for 4-5 hours on high until soft and easily pierced.

Soft & Smoky Roasted Peppers

As well as brightening up your meals, a pepper is a low-calorie vegetable full of nutritional benefits. In fact bell peppers are one of the top vegetables for providing vitamin C, vitamin A and carotenoids, which are important in maintaining eye and skin health.

This roasted pepper recipe is an incredibly simple one and offers a nice variation in texture from the usual raw bell pepper. Combine it with a wide variety of recipes, salads or simply serve as a side.

Prep Time: 5 minutes
Cook Time: 3 hours
Serves 4-5

1 tablespoon olive oil
4 red bell peppers, halved and seeded (you can try any peppers)

Method

Grease the slow cooker with the olive oil to avoid your peppers sticking. Place the peppers in the cooker flesh side up and cook on high for 3 hours. Check them occasionally to ensure they aren't sticking.

Once cooked, allow the peppers to cool and then separate the peel from the flesh. The peppers are then ready to serve as a side or to add to your favorite salads and dishes.

Easy Slow Cooker Tomato Puree (Passata)

Using your slow cooker to make your own tomato puree is a great way to create a recipe staple. Not only is making passata incredibly easy but you're also drastically reducing the amount of unnecessary ingredients if you were to use store-bought products.

This passata is ideal for everything from pasta sauces, to pizza bases and in lasagnas.

Prep Time: 5 minutes
Cook Time: 8 hours

Ingredients

12 plum tomatoes
1 tablespoon olive oil
1 teaspoon salt

Method

Remove the stems of the tomatoes and place the tomatoes into the cooker. Cook with the oil and salt for 8 hours on low.

Take the tomatoes out of the cooker with a slotted spoon. Then remove the liquid from the slow cooker. Put the tomatoes back in the cooker and blend until smooth.

Allow the mixture to cool and store either in the fridge or freezer.

Slow Cooker Cranberry Sauce

When Thanksgiving beckons there's usually very little space in the oven or on the stove, so utilizing your slow cooker wherever possible is a great way to free up space. This slow cooker cranberry sauce provides some great contrast and mild tartness to your meal. I guarantee you'll like it so much that you won't just be saving it for special occasions.

Prep Time: 5 minutes
Cook Time: 3-4 hours

12 ounce cranberries, fresh
½ cup orange juice
½ cup water
½ cup brown sugar
½ cup white sugar
¼ teaspoon ground cinnamon

Method

Combine all the ingredients in the slow cooker and stir. Cover and cook on high for 3 hours, stirring every hour.

Continue to cook until the sauce thickens and the majority of the cranberries have popped (usually between 3-4 hours).

Carefree Brown Rice

Rice is an ideal staple of any diet but tending to it on the stove can be a time-consuming and often inconsistent affair. To make your life a lot easier, why not instead use your slow cooker to make carefree brown rice, with any meal. Of course brown rice is also a lot more beneficial than white rice, as it is high in natural occurring oils, fiber and slow-release sugar.

Prep Time: 2 minutes
Cook Time: 2-3 hours

Serves 4-6

2 cups brown rice
5 cups water
Salt to season

Method

Combine all the ingredients in the slow cooker. Stir and place on the lid.

Cook for high for 2-3 hours without removing the lid, and serve.

Perfect Caramelized Onions

Caramelized onions are a delicious and versatile side that can be combined with a wide variety of dishes to help enhance their flavor. The options of what you can do with them are truly endless, from burgers, to putting them in salads and mashed potatoes. If you have onions that you don't want to waste, then this is your next recipe.

Prep Time: 5-10 minutes
Cook Time: 10 hours minimum
Serves 4-6

6+ onions, peeled and cut into half-moons
3 tablespoons butter, melted (or alternative)
2 tablespoons brown sugar
2 teaspoons balsamic vinegar
Salt and pepper

Method

Add the onions and butter to the slow cooker. Cook on low for 10 hours, stirring occasionally, until they begin to brown.

Add the remaining ingredients, stir well and continue to cook.

If there is too much liquid, then either sieve it out or leave the lid slightly off until it evaporates. Then check the onions regularly and cook until they have reached the point that you like them.

Allow the onions to cool and store for up to a week.

Easy Vegetable Stock

Vegetable stock is something you'll have noticed we use regularly in everything from soups to casseroles. While it is possible to buy jars or cubes of it, it is pretty easy to make your own and store it for when you need it! Every time you prepare vegetables, some of them will invariably go to waste, such as unwanted ends or stalks. These are the pieces that will make the foundation of a great vegetable stock.

Prep Time: 2 minutes
Cook Time: 7-8 hours

Any vegetable leftovers
2 bay leaves
Salt and pepper

Method

Every time you prepare vegetables, save any of the discarded peel, ends and stalks. These include the ends of onions, carrots, pieces of garlic, potato and much more.

Put these bits in freezer bags and store in your freezer until you have a full bag.

To make the stock, add the freezer bag contents to the slow cooker (still frozen) and cover with water. Add a few bay leaves, season with salt and pepper and heat on low for 7-8 hours.

Sieve the contents, removing the vegetables. Allow the stock to cool and place in containers to freeze or put in the fridge.

Luscious & Light Lemon Curd

Lemon curd is a versatile fruit spread that can be used in desserts, on toast and with yogurt. It's also pretty straightforward to make, and the low-cooking temperature of the slow cooker makes this even easier. You don't have to be limited by using lemons either! There are plenty of other fruits you can experiment with, so be sure to give them a go.

Prep Time: 5 minutes
Cook Time: 5 hours
Serves 4-6

2 eggs (or egg replacer)
8 tablespoons icing sugar
6 tablespoons lemon juice, freshly squeezed
2 tablespoons butter (or dairy-free alternative), softened
½ teaspoon ginger, fresh, grated (keep the juice)
Small pinch of salt
Cold water

Method

In a medium bowl, beat the ingredients together. The butter might not mix fully but this is fine.

Divide the mixture into individual ramekins and pop them into the slow cooker. Fill the cooker with cold water, around ¾ the way up the ramekins sides.

Cover them with foil, put the cover on and cook on low for 5 hours. Stir the mixtures occasionally throughout the cooking time.

Once the curd has thickened and sticks to a spoon, it is ready. Note: it will also thicken when it cools.

Scrumptious Strawberry Jam

This slow cooker jam is a great addition to toast, sponge cakes and oatmeal. Use strawberries or experiment with other in season fruit. When jarred it even makes for a wonderful gift!

Prep Time: 5-10 minutes
Cook Time: 10 hours

4 pounds fresh strawberries
3 cups sugar
2-3.5 ounces pectin powder (can use HTF sugar-free version)

Method

Wash the strawberries and remove the stems. Quarter and place into the slow cooker.

Mash the strawberries with a potato masher in order to create juice, and then add the sugar and pectin.

Stir further, mashing more if you see fit.

Cover and cook for 10 hours on low. If the berries aren't sticking together how you'd like, then add more pectin to thicken and cook for longer.

Nice & Easy Slow Cooker Chickpeas

Cooking chickpeas in the slow cooker is a great way to enjoy this legume without any hassle. There's no worry about water boiling, and the beans are less likely to split apart. Packed full of protein, chickpeas make a great vegan-friendly snack and their high fiber content makes them ideal for snacking on. Eat them as a snack or incorporate into your favorite salad or casserole.

Prep Time: 2 minutes
Cook Time: 3 hours
Serves 3 cups

1 cup dried chickpeas
32 ounces vegetable broth or water
½ onion, peeled but otherwise left whole
1 teaspoon salt

Method

Soak overnight before cooking (not necessary if you've forgotten). Rinse well and transfer to the slow cooker with the other ingredients.

Cover and cook on high for 3 hours or until the peas are tender. Drain, remove the onion and enjoy.

Ginger Lemon Hot Toddies

If you're looking for the perfect drink to sooth a sore throat, then the ginger lemon hot toddy is for you. Typically made with alcohol (which you're free to add or remove), the hot toddy combines soothing honey and remedying ginger to nurse away any signs of a cold.

Prep Time: 5 minutes
Cook Time: 4 hours

4 cups water
1 cups lemon juice, fresh
1 cup honey
2½ tablespoons ginger, crystallized, finely chopped
½ ginger, whole, peeled, fresh, cut into ¼-inch-thick slices
4 cloves, whole
¼ cup rum, golden (optional)
¼ cup brandy (optional)

Method

Add all the ingredients except the alcohol in the slow cooker. Cook for 4 hours.

Discard the ginger slices. Stir in the alcohol and serve.

Chex Mix

Chex mix is an all-time favorite that doubles up as both a great snack and as a breakfast option when you're on the move. It provides a salty, crunchy, savory treat that is perfect for snacking.

Feel free to sub in whatever ingredients you have at hand – from cereals to crackers and even cookies.

Prep Time: 5-10 minutes
Cook Time: 3 hours
Serves 6-8

8 cups Chex cereal
2 cups pretzels
1 cup peanuts
⅓ cup butter, melted and hot
1 tablespoon seasoned salt
¼ cup Worcestershire sauce

Method

Add the cereal, pretzels and peanuts to the slow cooker.

Mix the butter, salt, and Worcestershire sauce in a bowl.

Pour the dressing over the cereal mixture; mix thoroughly for a 1-2 minutes. Cover and cook on low for 3 hours, stirring occasionally so the mixture doesn't burn. Leave a gap in your slow cooker's lid to prevent condensation from forming and softening the mix.

Allow the mixture to cool on a baking sheet. Serve or store for up to 3 weeks.

Curried Roasted Almonds

Almonds are packed full of healthy fats, proteins and fiber, making them an ideal snack. The addition of curry powder adds a spicy note that complements the sweetness of the almonds.

Prep Time: 5 minutes
Cook Time: 4 hours
Serves 4-6

2 tablespoons melted butter
1 tablespoon curry powder
½ teaspoon seasoning salt
1 pound blanched almonds

Method

Mix the melted butter, curry powder and salt together. Add the almonds to the slow cooker and pour over the mixture.

Cover and cook on low for 2-3 hours. Uncover the slow cooker and turn to high, cook for another hour.

Vanilla Hazelnut Creamer

If you're a coffee fan but want to control the amount of hidden sugar you're consuming from your daily hit, then try this creamer recipe. The vanilla hazelnut creamer is super thick and rich, and uses only a few ingredients to create such a full flavor.

You can make it unsweetened or add a little natural sweetener if you prefer — either way you'll be making your own artisan coffee a lot sooner than you think.

Prep Time: 10 minutes
Cook Time: 7-8 hours

1½ cups water
1 cup whole hazelnuts
½ vanilla bean, cut lengthwise
1 teaspoon vanilla extract
Sweetener of your choice (optional)

Method

Add all the ingredients except the sweetener to the slow cooker. Cook on low for 7-8 hours. Pour the contents into a blender and blend until smooth. Add your preferred sweetener and blend again.

You can store the creamer for up to a week in the fridge and add to any of your coffee or hot chocolate drinks for an extra rich treat.

Conclusion

I hope you have enjoyed looking through my vegetarian slow cooker recipes. A lot of time and love has gone into testing and modifying these recipes, ensuring they aren't just delicious but simple to make and full of healthy ingredients.

Slow cookers are a fantastic way to introduce you and your loved ones to ingredients that you might have either been intimidated or reluctant to try. Beans, lentils and legumes are a perfect example of this; I know how daunting and time consuming it can be to cook them on stove. But slow cookers allow you to just drop them in, turn on the heat and come back when they are perfectly cooked.

All of these recipes can be adapted, so feel free to substitute different ingredients in and out to make a recipe your own. Just try out some of the recipes and you'll be wondering how you ever managed before!

Above all, I hope my slow cooker recipes help you maintain a healthy and wholefoods based diet so you look and feel at your absolute best. Take care of your slow cooker and it will take care of you.

58763045R00105

Made in the USA
Lexington, KY
17 December 2016